PAUL
THE MAN

His Life and Work

PAUL Blinded
ACTS 9:4-9
22: 13-16 RENAMED

Books by Clarence Edward Macartney

Great Women of the Bible
The Greatest Texts of the Bible
Paul the Man

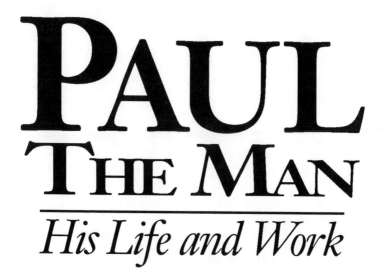

PAUL
THE MAN
His Life and Work

Clarence Edward Macartney

kregel PUBLICATIONS

Grand Rapids, MI 49501

Paul the Man: His Life and His Ministry, by Clarence Edward Macartney, © 1992 by Kregel Publications, P.O. Box 2607, Grand Rapids, Michigan 49501. This edition includes minor changes in the text, insertion of subheads, and arrangement of the sermons.

Cover painting: *The Apostle Paul* by Rembrandt, *c.* 1635, Kunsthistorifchet Museum, Vienna
Cover and book design: Alan G. Hartman

Library of Congress Cataloging-in-Publication Data

Macartney, Clarence Edward Noble, 1879-1957.

Paul the man: his life and his ministry / Clarence Edward Macartney.
  p. cm.
 Reprint. Originally published: New York: Fleming H. Revell, 1947.
  1. Paul, the Apostle, Saint. 2. Christian saints—Turkey—Tarsus—Biography. 3. Tarsus (Turkey)—Biography. I. Title.
BS2506.M25   1992 225.9'2—dc20 92-16135
                     CIP

ISBN 0-8254-3269-3

    1 2 3 4 5 year / printing 96 95 94 93 92

Printed in the United States of America

CONTENTS

PUBLISHER'S PREFACE

For twenty-seven years Dr. Charles Edward Noble Macartney pastored the influential First Presbyterian Church of Pittsburgh, Pennsylvania. Prior to that pastorate he ministered in Paterson, New Jersey, and Philadelphia, Pennsylvania. His preaching especially attracted men, not only to his Sunday services but also to his popular noon luncheons. Because of his skill and eloquence in expounding the lives of Bible characters, he was well-called "the American Alexander Whyte." Still, his preaching was always biblical, doctrinal and practical, albeit topical-textual in approach.

This collection of sermons on the Apostle Paul first appeared in 1947, published by Fleming H. Revell. An earlier edition was published by Williams and Norgate Ltd. of London, England, in 1929. It represents a unique look at the church of Jesus Christ's first and foremost missionary. Except for slight modifications and updating, and the insertion of Scripture references, these sermons are reissued in their original form. It is the publisher's prayer that they will encourage today's preachers and teachers.

1

THE MAN AND HIS AGE

The life and ministry of our Lord Jesus Christ upon earth was preceded and followed by the life and work of a great man. Of these two men, John the Baptist was the greatest man before Christ and St. Paul the greatest man after Christ. John the Apostle, writing of John the Baptist, said of him, "There was a man sent from God whose name was John." If we substitute the name Paul for John, and make the sentence read, "There was a man sent from God whose name was Paul," we have the shortest and most satisfactory biography of St. Paul. In his labors, his travels, in his sermons and writings, in his trials and imprisonments and death, that is the sentence which always confronts us, "A man sent from God."

The most eloquent of Christian preachers in the most eloquent tribute ever paid to St. Paul called him, "The heart of the world." What we shall do in these pages will be to feel the pulses of that mighty heart as it beats for us in the pages of the New Testament and in the life of the world today. The great men of the past have appeared in the great crises or turning points of history. They cannot be separated from their day and generation, and their greatness is in part the greatness of the age in which they lived. St. Paul is no exception to this rule. He appears upon the stage of human affairs at a great epoch. Jesus Christ had come and preached and died and risen again from the dead and ascended into heaven, leaving to His disciples the work of preaching the Gospel to all the world. In this great work the foremost place was to be taken by one who not only was not of the original followers of Christ, but who was the chief enemy of Christ and of His Church. How strange are the ways of God. Out of the ranks of the haters and adversaries of Christ God chooses Saul of Tarsus to carry the story of Christ and Him crucified to the nations of the world. Human wisdom and planning would never have chosen such a man. But the ways of God are not the ways of man, and it was the fierce, persecuting hater of Christ and His disciples whom God called to be a "chosen vessel" to bear His name before nations and kings and the children of Israel.

AN EXAMPLE OF CHRISTIAN CHARACTER

After Christ Himself and the Scriptures, St. Paul is the greatest possession of the Christian Church. In St. Paul Christianity gained four great things. First, an incomparable example of Christian character. To Christians in Corinth Paul once wrote, "Be ye followers of me even as I am also of Christ." We are not shocked at this invitation on the part of a man, asking other men to imitate and follow him, because we know that no man ever followed Christ so faithfully. Even if we had no record of the life of Christ in the Four Gospels, the life of Paul as we have it in the pages of the Acts and the Epistles would be sufficient to show us the glory of the Christian life and the way to follow Christ. Second, in St. Paul Christianity secured a great thinker. Nothing is so rare as a really great mind. St. Paul was such a mind. His mind not only entertains great ideas and kindles with high enthusiasms, but it was a logical, searching, analytical mind. He is not content to declare that the Christ of the Cross is the ground of our forgiveness, but he shows why and how that death is the satisfaction for our sins. To this one great fact, the death of Christ and its meaning for the human race. St. Paul devoted all the powers of his wonderful intellect. How great the influence of that mind was, is witnessed to even by the enemies of Christ and the Gospel, when they tell us, as they are telling us today, that St. Paul was the founder and the inventor of the religion which centers around the Cross of Christ. The charge is false and preposterous, yet it pays an extraordinary tribute to the greatness of the mind of Paul.

In the third place, Christianity gained in St. Paul a great preacher and missionary and church builder. In him intellectual gifts were united with practical gifts of the highest sort. We hardly know at which to wonder the more, his grand utterances concerning the Christian faith and hope, or the way in which he could deal with all kinds and conditions of men and meet all kinds of situations. He is always at home and at ease and able to cope with the situation, whether addressing the mob before the castle in Jerusalem, speaking before the Sanhedrin, disputing in the synagogues, speaking to the philosophers on Mars Hill, exhorting the peasants of the mountains of Galatia, pleading his case before Festus, Agrippa and Felix, or encouraging the despairing passengers and crew on the sinking grain ship off the coast of Malta. Together with this amazing adaptability and versatility went an equally amazing and never flagging energy, enthusiasm, and joy. In the prosecution of his task he has a noble disregard for difficulties and a willingness to endure all things for the sake of Christ. So possessed was he with devotion to the cause of Christ, that he could truthfully say, "It is no longer I that live, but Christ liveth in me." Although he was intensely human, sensitive to all the sorrows and pains of mortal experience, there are times when we seem to be following the history of one who was lifted out of the ordinary by his complete devotion to God's will in his life.

In the fourth place, Christianity gained in St. Paul a mighty evidence of the truth of the Gospel. The greatest evidence for the truth of the Gospel is the resurrection of Christ from the dead. Christians point to the empty grave and know that Christ was the Son of God. But after the resurrection itself, the most powerful evidence for the truth of Christianity is the life and ministry of St. Paul. The weight of this evidence has been felt in all ages, and is as powerful and significant today as ever before. Because Saul of Tarsus, the fierce bigot, blasphemer and persecutor became Paul the Apostle, Christ's noblest friend and advocate, and the chief destroyer and waster of the churches the chief builder of them, and because from the mind of this former enemy of Christ comes the greater part of the New Testament, the most profound statement of Christian truth, the most beautiful and winsome presentation of the Christian graces and virtues, we can believe in the ultimate triumph of the Church of Christ and that the gates of Hell shall not prevail against it.

ANOTHER CHILD

About the time that a mother's heart rejoiced over the child which lay on her breast in the manger at Bethlehem, another mother in far-off Tarsus held in her arms of love another child whom his parents called Saul. Two infants in their mothers' arms. But one was destined to be the world's Savior and Redeemer, and the other to be His great apostle. In the mysterious purposes of God the star which halted over the manger at Bethlehem whispers concerning the future to the star which halted over the house of the Pharisee in Tarsus.

Tarsus was an important town in its day. Paul was proud of his birthplace and described himself as a "citizen of no mean city." It was the capital and chief city of the Roman province of Cilicia in south-east Asia Minor, and was situated on the river Cydnus, not far from the sea. It was at Tarsus that Cleopatra, the charmer of the Nile, came to meet and to conquer Marc Antony with her witchery. Near Tarsus, too, at Issus, Alexander the Great won a great victory over Darius three centuries before Christ. Back of Tarsus was the famous pass, the Gates of Cilicia, through which the caravans of commerce and trade and the armies of conquerors entered into or came out of central Asia Minor. Neither in connection with Tarsus, nor in connection with any other of the great cities and beautiful regions which he visited, does St. Paul mention or describe the architecture of the place or the wonders of sea and mountain and plain.

Someone has wondered that John Calvin could have spent so much time in Geneva and yet had never a word to say about the lake and the mountains upon which he daily looked. The reason was probably the same as in the case of Paul, that the intensity of his great spiritual and moral purpose burned up every other thought. But where Paul is silent others have spoken, and from their accounts we know that the country about Tarsus with its rugged snow-covered mountains in the background and its rushing river and its fields covered with rich green in the springtime, was one of unusual beauty. Tarsus was a free city, that is, governed by its magistrates and exempted from military occupation. Its citizens were Jews, Greeks and Cilicians, and its university was one of the most famous in the world. This busy commercial city then, with its mixed population and its celebrated university was the cradle of St. Paul, in striking contrast with little Nazareth where Jesus was brought up.

As to Paul's family we know almost nothing. His father was a Pharisee, for Paul describes himself as a Pharisee and a son of Pharisees. The denunciation by our Lord of the Pharisees has made the name almost a synonym for bigotry and hypocrisy. But we must remember that they were not all whited sepulchres, and, as in the case of Gamaliel and Nicodemus, represented the most honorable and the most deeply religious of the different groups among the Jews. We should like to know something about Paul's mother, for we may be sure that like nearly every remarkable man Paul must have had an unusual mother. But there is no reference on the part of Paul to the mother who bore him. In the Letter to the Romans, where he sends greetings to friends and relatives, Paul sends a message to one Rufus, "Salute Rufus, chosen in the Lord, and his mother and mine." And mine? What does Paul mean by that? Was the mother of Rufus one who had been kind to Paul and taken the part of a mother toward him? All we can say is that the mother of Rufus is singled out by Paul for honorable mention which gives her an immortality of fame.

In this same letter Paul names others who were his kinsmen, Andronicus, Junias, Herodion, Lucius, Jason and Sosipater. We have a reference, too, to his sister, whose son, then a young man, saved him from death at Jerusalem by informing him of the plot against his life and then notifying the chief captain.

Since Paul's family was of the tribe of Benjamin, it was natural that he should have been given the name of Israel's first king who was of the tribe of Benjamin, Saul. This name Saul bears until the time of the conversion of Sergius Paulus at Cyprus, after which he is spoken of as Paul. Jacob's blessing upon his son Benjamin used to be taken as a prophecy of the history of Paul, his persecuting fury before he became a Christian and his service to the Church after his conversion. "Benjamin is a wolf that raveneth: in the morning he shall devour the prey, and at even he shall divide the spoil." Like all Hebrew boys, Paul was taught a trade, that of the tent-maker. This craftsmanship served him in good stead in after years and on more than one occasion we find Paul either living with those who were of this trade, as in the case of Aquila and Priscilla, or, as at Thessalonica, supporting himself with his own hands.

A BLAMELESS YOUTH

Some of the most eminent servants of God have had to look back upon a youth of sin and dissipation. The Confessions of the great St. Augustine make sad reading in this respect. But St. Paul's youth was blameless. He says that as touching the righteousness which is in the law he was found blameless, and on another occasion that he knew "nothing against himself." Unlike many another, Paul did not require to utter the prayer of David, "Remember not the sins of my youth, nor my transgressions." When the light of Christ shone into his heart Paul declared himself to be the chief of sinners. But we have reason to believe that his youth and manhood were free from the stain of gross immorality. He was indeed a "chosen vessel," but the vessel which God chose to carry the Gospel was a clean one.

Brought up in the home of a Pharisee, Paul was well trained in the Old Testament and in Jewish customs and laws. In his childhood he laid the foundations of that complete knowledge of the Old Testament Scriptures which he possessed in common with Him whose Gospel he was one day to preach. Parents, friends, or the rabbi noted something unusual about this boy Saul and suggested that he be trained for a rabbi.

This, then, became the goal and ambition of his life, and at an early age he was sent up to Jerusalem to be trained under the celebrated teacher and Pharisee, Gamaliel. Paul says he sat at the feet of Gamaliel; probably a literal fact. He learned great lessons from the famous doctor of the Old Testament, but certainly not the lesson of persecuting fury, for it was Gamaliel who, when the people were about to stone Peter and John, warned them to refrain from violence, saying, "Refrain from these men and let them alone, for if this counsel or this work be of men it will come to naught: but if it be of God, ye cannot overthrow it; lest haply ye be found to fight against God." There in the holy city of David, surrounded by the memorials of Israel's greatness and often entering the temple of Herod, the young Saul of Tarsus prepared himself to teach the law and forward the cause of Israel in the world, little dreaming that he was being fitted to preach the Gospel of the despised Nazarene.

We wonder if in these days at Jerusalem, Saul ever caught a glimpse of that other youth from Nazareth whose heart too was kindling with great desires for Israel and the world. When the lad from Nazareth stood before the doctors in the Temple, both hearing them and asking them questions, was the lad from Tarsus present, and did he wonder at the questions of the lad from Nazareth?

Paul's father at Tarsus was a Roman citizen, for Paul declared that he was Roman-born. This fact was a most important one in his subsequent career, as we shall see when Paul starts on his missionary journeys. Roman citizenship exempted the holder from degrading punishment and gave him the right of appeal to the Roman Emperor. In his hour of need Paul availed himself of both these privileges. In a remarkable way, therefore, this man who was to evangelize the nations is prepared for his task by the very circumstances of his birth and early surroundings. He is a Hebrew of the Hebrews, but born in a Greek city where he learned the Greek tongue, and yet a Roman citizen and under Roman dominion. Israel, Greece and Rome place their hands upon him in the days of his youth.

PAUL'S WORLD

What of the world and the age into which Paul was born? Politically the world was Roman, and that vast empire stretched from the Atlantic Ocean on the west to the Euphrates on the east, and from the Danube and the Rhine on the north to the Nile and the deserts of Africa and Arabia on the south. The Roman conquest and peace had brought a degree of prosperity and industry. But underneath that surface of world peace was a sea of discontent and unhappiness and an abyss of moral degradation. Half the population of Rome was slave. There were rights for Romans, but the rights of man as such were not recognized; that came only with the spread of the Christian conception of human nature and the human family. Side by side with the splendor and prosperity of Rome, there went the pauperizing and brutalizing of the masses, the decay of public virtue and the decline of marriage and the home. The old faiths and cults seemed to be played out and skepticism and atheism were rampant. Tacitus, one of the Roman historians, in describing the age, says he will take us only as far as the mouth of the foul cavern of Roman society lest the noxious fumes destroy us. To know the moral condition of the world we need only to read the terrible account of it in Paul's Letter to the Romans. It was a world sunk in wickedness and despair, a world without hope and without God.

Paul speaks twice of the Gospel as being preached in the "fullness of times." In a very striking way the world had been prepared for the preaching of the ever-lasting Gospel. In this preparation we may note four chief factors. First, the dispersion of the Jews. They were scattered throughout the Roman world, and wherever Paul goes to preach the Gospel he finds a synagogue which he can enter and which gives him a platform for the proclamation of Christ. Where the Jews come today, the churches prepare to move out. But we must remember that when the Gospel was first preached it was the fact of the presence of the Jews and their synagogue which made the apostles feel that they could make an impression upon the people; for the Jews were trained to the belief in one God over all, and they had been taught to expect the Messiah and the fulfillment of the Old Testament prophecies.

A second factor in the preparation of the world for Christ was the spread of the Greek language. This had been accomplished through the conquests of Alexander the Great, who made Greek the world tongue. The Gospels were written in Greek and St. Paul was himself well versed in the Greek language, so much so that he could get a hearing in Athens itself.

A third important factor was the vast system of Roman roads. From a golden milestone in the midst of the Roman Forum, great highways, such as the Appian and the Egnatian, radiated to all parts of the Roman Empire. It is safe to say that the means of transportation were faster and safer in the age of St. Paul than in any subsequent age until the nineteenth century, with the invention of the steam engine. These splendid roads had been made for the feet of those who came to publish the good tidings of peace and forgiveness through Jesus Christ.

Last of all, in this providential preparation, the crowning factor in the "fullness of times," was the world-wide unity of the Roman Empire. This political unity was a sort of mould into which the apostles poured their great conception of the unity and universality of the Christian faith, a kingdom as wide as the human family and in which Jesus Christ was king over all.

2

SHADOWS OF COMING EVENTS

We first see the face of St. Paul in the light of the fierce passions which raged at the stoning of Stephen, the first of the noble army of the martyrs. Paul appears on the stage of Christian history just in time to hear the first martyr pray, " Lord Jesus, receive my spirit." He passes from the stage of Christian history with the same kind of prayer on his lips and with Stephen's great expectation in his heart: "I am now ready to be offered up. Henceforth, there is laid up for me a crown of righteousness which the Lord, the righteous judge, will give me at that day." Between those two farewells, the farewell of Stephen, spoken with bleeding lips, and with Paul urging on those who hurled the stones, and the farewell of Paul, written in the damp and gloom of the Mamertine dungeon, lies the great miracle of Christian history, the conversion of Saul.

Behold these two faces, the face of the martyr and the face of the persecutor and inquisitor. Cut to the heart by the accusation of Stephen before the Council, that they had betrayed and murdered the Just One, whose coming had been foretold by the prophets, the members of the Sanhedrin stopped their ears and with a wild cry of fanatical rage ran on Stephen and dragged him out of the city to stone him. The Old Testament law required that if a man were condemned to death, those who had witnessed against him should take part in his execution. These were the witnesses who laid their clothes at the young man's feet, whose name was Saul, for their flowing garments would have impeded the swing of their arms as they hurled the stones. As we look on that scene those two faces stand out above the others. We see Stephen kneeling in prayer amid the shower of stones and the rain of curses. His face is stained with blood; but as he looks up steadfastly into heaven, that face is transfigured with the reflection of the glory which he beheld, Jesus, standing at the right hand of God. The stains of blood, the imprint of the cruel stones, the marks of emaciation and imprisonment and all the lineaments of our weak mortality seem to fade and disappear, and in their place we see as it were the face of an angel.

THE FACES OF TWO MEN

When we turn our gaze from the dying martyr to the raging mob who hurl the curses and the stones, we forget the crowd as we are caught and held by the face of one man. He is a young man about twenty-eight years of age. At his feet lie a heap of garments, those which the witnesses have laid there. This face too is lighted up as with a burning flame, but it is the light of zeal for the law of Israel and anger for him who claimed that the crucified Galilean impostor Jesus was the great Messiah of the prophets, and had called the members of Israel's council "betrayers and murderers." Although not throwing the stones himself, by word and by excited gesture the young rabbi incited the mob to their brutal work. Every stone which hits its mark and draws a groan or a drop of blood from Stephen, draws an exclamation of delight from the fierce young zealot. By and by, the prayer of Stephen grows fainter and fainter, until it is heard no longer. The bleeding and battered head falls lower and lower on the breast, and at length the body of Stephen lies motionless on the ground, covered with the heap of stones. The witnesses take up their garments which they had laid at the feet of Saul, who congratulates them upon their vindication of the honor of Israel and the glory of the Messiah.

Who, looking down upon the actors in that tragedy outside the walls of Jerusalem, would have dared to predict that one day that fierce young doctor of the law, his form vibrating with excitement, and his arm and voice raised in approval and encouragement of those who did the wrong, will be Christ's greatest lover and chiefest apostle? But the Holy Ghost, looking down upon that awful scene, saw the fierce light in the face of Saul, and said, "Him will I have for a chosen vessel to bear the name of Christ to the kingdoms and nations of the earth." One day another martyr was led out from the dungeon near the Roman Forum and conducted to a spot outside the walls of the city, near where the pyramid of Caius Caestius stands today. The headman's sword flashed for a second in the bright Italian sun, and that young man, now old, whom we had seen inciting the mob at the stoning of Stephen, has gone to be with Christ and to seek the forgiveness of Stephen, and together with Stephen sing praises unto Him for whom both of them had died. Truly, God works in a mysterious way His wonders to perform.

> "Deep in unfathomable mines
> Of never-failing skill,
> He treasures up His bright designs
> And works His sovereign will."

This astounding change in the life of Saul of Tarsus was brought about through his seeing what Stephen saw when he was dying, the glory of God, and Jesus standing on the right hand of God. He saw Jesus, and his life was turned over as if by an earthquake. But before we come to the recital of that great transformation, we must recall some of the things which have taken place since the ascension of Jesus, and watch the shadows of coming events.

THE COMING OF THE COMFORTER

Before He was taken up into heaven, Christ told the disciples that they were to be His witnesses unto the uttermost parts of the earth, but charged them to tarry in Jerusalem until they had received power through the coming of the Holy Ghost. This instruction to "wait for the promise of the Father" was in keeping with what Christ had said before His death about sending the Comforter. All that the coming of the Holy Ghost meant they could not have surmised until the mighty event itself. The period of waiting they employed in prayer and fellowship and supplication. During this time also, and under the leadership of Peter who, restored and forgiven by Christ, had resumed his old place in the apostolic band, the disciples chose Matthias as a successor to Judas, who "went to his own place."

Then on the day of Pentecost, the birthday of the Church, as they were all with one accord in one place, with a mighty rushing wind and with the appearance of tongues as of fire, the Holy Ghost descended upon them and they all began to speak with other tongues as the Spirit gave them utterance. At this feast of Pentecost Jerusalem was filled with devout Jews and proselytes from all parts of the world, and these men, Parthians, Medes, Elamites, dwellers in Mesopotamia, Cappadocia, Pontus and Asia, Phrygia, Pamphylia, the Libyan deserts of Africa, Egypt, Cretans, Arabians and men from Rome, were amazed and startled to hear the apostles preaching the works of God in their own tongue. What happened was a grand prophecy of the spread of the Gospel, and the man who was to take the leading part in that world-wide dissemination of the Gospel was not yet on the horizon. Perhaps he was one of those who scoffed at the preaching of the disciples and said, "These men are full of new wine." In answer to this charge Peter arose and delivered the great sermon which converted three thousand souls.

With daily additions to the Church through the preaching of the Word, the next event of importance was the healing of the lame man by Peter at the Gate Beautiful of the temple. The miracle was followed by another great sermon, which was interrupted by the Sadducees, who were particularly incensed at the prominence given by Peter's preaching to the doctrine of the resurrection. At their instigation Peter and John were haled before the scribes and rulers and the high priest, the same who had presided at the trial of Jesus. After sternly warning the two apostles that they should no longer speak to the people in "this name," that is, the name of Jesus, the rulers let them go.

Peter and John paid no heed to the warning, declaring, as the pioneers of Christian liberty of conscience, that they would obey God rather than man. Again arrested, they were delivered out of the prison by the Angel of the Lord, and straightway proceeded to the temple where they began to preach again. The angry leaders of the Jews were cut to the heart and took counsel how to kill these disturbers of the peace. They would have carried out their

design had it not been for the intervention of the renowned
Gamaliel, Saul's preceptor, who persuaded them to refrain from
violence, saying that if this work of the Galilean fanatic was of
man it would come to nothing anyway, but if it was of God they
could not overthrow it. This secured for the infant Church a
much needed period of rest and security, during which the Gospel was proclaimed and converts added to the Church.

In the dramatic story of Ananias and Sapphira we hear of the
Christian communism which was established at Jerusalem and
which, no doubt, helped to preserve the struggling Church. Here,
too, in the deceit of Ananias, who kept back a part of the money
he had received for his property, we have the appearance of what
is now so sadly familiar to us all, the tares in the midst of the
wheat, the evil mixed with the good in the Church.

Another stage in the growth of the Christian community at Jerusalem was the establishment of a body of seven deacons, who were
charged with the distribution of the charities of the Church, in
order that the apostles themselves might be left free to preach the
Gospel. Of these seven, two, Philip and Stephen, soon went beyond
their particular commission and became powerful preachers of the
Word. Stephen, "full of faith and power," did great wonders and
miracles among the people, entering into the synagogues and disputing with the Jews. One of these synagogues was that attended by
Jews from Cilicia, Saul's native province. As the devout Stephen
reasoned with them about Jesus and the Old Testament prophecies,
we can imagine the young doctor of the law from Tarsus, listening
with scorn and righteous indignation in his face. What blasphemy
and outrage! Here in the synagogue itself, and to Jews versed in the
Scriptures, to declare that a crucified malefactor and impostor was
the glorious Messiah of Israel! Although no record is preserved, we
doubt not that Saul was foremost among those who charged Stephen with blasphemy, on which charge he was condemned and, as
we have seen, executed.

The stoning of Stephen stirred up again all the persecuting fury
which had been held in check for a little period by Gamaliel's
counsel of toleration. "And at that time there was a great persecution against the Church," Saul himself taking the lead and making
havoc of the Church, dragging the followers of Jesus out of their
houses into prison. The apostles remained in Jerusalem and braved

the fury of the storm; but most of the converts at Jerusalem were scattered abroad. But God made the wrath of man to praise Him. By driving the Christians out of Jerusalem the enemies of the Gospel only gave it a wider circulation, for wherever they went in their flight from the persecution of Saul, the converts of yesterday proved their worth and genuineness by preaching the Word. Most conspicuous among these preachers was the deacon Philip, who went down to despised Samaria, thus fulfilling the last command of Jesus that His disciples were to be His witnesses in Samaria. His success at Samaria brought Peter and John down to the same city to confirm and establish what Philip had commenced. Here at Samaria too occurred the dramatic incident of the judgment upon the sorcerer, Simon, who, seeing the miracles wrought by Philip and the apostles, offered them money for the gift of the Holy Spirit. To him Peter answered, "Thy money perish with thee, because thou hast thought that the gift of God may be purchased with money."

After his mission at Samaria, Philip was the means of converting perhaps the first notable personage from the outside world, the Ethiopian eunuch, chancellor of Candace, Queen of the Ethiopians. It is interesting to note also that what won him to Christ was Philip's interpretation of the fifty-third chapter of Isaiah as fulfilled in Christ.

The persecutors at Jerusalem viewed with dismay and anger the rapid spread of the Gospel and noted how all the regions round about Jerusalem were embracing the odious heresy. In ancient Damascus particularly, there was a numerous and thriving company of Christians. It was clear to the enemies of the Gospel that new measures must be devised. It was of no avail to crush the heresy at Jerusalem and permit it to thrive elsewhere. They must proceed against the dangerous and blasphemous doctrine wherever it had taken root. To this end, Saul of Tarsus, now recognized as the thief of the inquisitors and persecutors, armed with a commission from the high priest which gave him authority to arrest and bring to Jerusalem for trial any whom he found of "the way," set out for Damascus on the memorable journey which was to have such unexpected and momentous results, taking captivity captive, and making the fierce persecutor himself forever afterwards the "prisoner of Jesus Christ."

3

THE BLOW OF GOD

W hen Elijah told Naaman the leper to go and wash himself seven times in Jordan, that indignant and mortified prime minister, thinking of the rivers of his native Damascus, exclaimed, "Are not the waters of Abana and Pharpar, rivers of Damascus, better than all the waters in Israel?" The amazement and anger of Naaman will be understood and appreciated by the traveler who makes his approach to the world's oldest inhabited city by the road over which furious Saul of Tarsus passed on his way to persecute the Church at Damascus.

If Egypt is the gift of the Nile, Damascus and the fertile country round about it are the gift of Abana and Pharpar, the two crystal streams which flow around the city like a lover's arm. To the west rises the snowy peak of Hermon, where Jesus was transfigured; to the east and northeast the graceful summits of a range of hills, and between them and the city the still cool waters of the Lake of the Meadow. In the midst of the fertile plain, like a diamond set in emeralds, lies Damascus, the Eye of the East. The domes and minarets of Islam did not then rise over the ancient town, but the same white flat-roofed houses were there, and the same gardens with their luxuriant tangle of fruits and flowers, with the cool waters drawn from the Abana laving the garden walls; the olive and the cypress trees were just as green, the leaves of the tall poplars just as white and glistening, and the pomegranate and walnut as graceful and as fruitful; the sky above just as clear and deep and blue. No wonder that when the Arab dreamed of Paradise his imagery was drawn from the groves and gardens and cooling streams of Damascus.

PAUL IN DAMASCUS

This panorama of beauty was spread out before Saul of Tarsus when, on the third day of his journey from Jerusalem, at high noon, he drew nigh to Damascus. But Saul had no eye for that fair picture which has drawn a sigh from the breast of the traveler of every age. He saw it not, for his heart was hot with the furious passion of persecution which had brought him to Damascus. The hour of noon in the east is the hour when men pause in their journeys and in the shade of the trees seek refuge from the intolerable rays of the sun. But Saul of Tarsus hurries on. There was Damascus, his goal, and there, little dreaming that their cruel foe was at hand, dwelt the humble followers of the Nazarene. Like the hunter who sees his prey not far off, the eye of Saul gleamed with fierce delight and his breast heaved with excitement.

But Saul was not destined to enter Damascus as the foe of Christ. He, who on yonder Hermon put on for a little the glory which he had with God the Father before His amazed and frightened disciples, was keeping watch over Damascus and over Saul of Tarsus. Suddenly, a blinding dazzling light flashed out of the blue sky, and Saul and his companions fell to the earth as if smitten by a stroke of lightning. Then all heard a voice, but Saul alone understood what was said. "Saul, Saul, why persecutest thou me?" The atonished persecutor replied, "Who art thou, Lord?" And the Lord said, "I am Jesus, whom thou persecutest."

Saul did not know that he was persecuting Jesus. Jesus the Galilean impostor was crucified, dead and buried. That, Saul was convinced, was the end of Him. He was not persecuting Him, but the ignorant fools and fanatics who said He was the Messiah and told tales of His rising from the grave and of His coming back one day to the earth. But now he learns that it is Jesus whom he is persecuting. Jesus identifies Himself with His people.

Who persecutes His followers persecutes Him. Scotland has given many martyrs to the Church and to civil liberty, but there is no tale of martyrdom which so touches a Scottish heart as that of the two Wigtown martyrs, Mary and Agnes Wilson, who perished in the Solway tide. The elder sister was fastened to a stake much further out than the younger, with the thought that when the younger saw the sufferings and death struggles of her sister she would recant. Quickly the inexorable tide of the Solway came in, first to the ankles, then to the knees, then to the waist, then to the neck, then to the lips. The executioners called to the younger sister, "Look! What seest thou?" Turning her head a little, she saw the struggles of her drowning sister, and then made her calm answer, "What do I see? I see the Lord Jesus suffering in one of His members!" So it was Christ who suffered in the victims of Saul's persecutions.

Amazed, startled, yet certain that he was face to face with Christ, Saul said, "Lord, what wilt thou have me to do?" The answer was, "Arise, go into the city, and it shall be told thee what thou must do." Then Saul, blinded by the glory he had seen, arose from the earth, and he who had come near to Damascus breathing out threatening and slaughter against the followers of Jesus, now entered the city, weak, blinded, led by the hand like a child, forever now the prisoner of Jesus Christ.

FROM PERSECUTOR TO PREACHER

That this great change took place in the life of Saul of Tarsus, that, as the Christians of Judea afterwards testified, "He that persecuted us in times past, now preacheth the faith which once he destroyed," no man doubts. Every effect has a corresponding and sufficient cause. What, then, was the cause of this mighty effect, the changing of a cruel enemy and persecutor into a loving friend and apostle? Some have tried to account for this great transformation on purely natural grounds. They say that Saul suffered a sunstroke. The blazing heat of the desert over which he had passed and the defiance of the usual laws of noon time rest had been too much for him. A sunstroke under such circumstances is quite conceivable. But since when did sunstrokes give a man a vision of the risen Christ and turn persecutors into apostles? Others have said that there must have been a sudden thunderstorm, and this, working on Saul's conscience, frightened him and he became convinced that he should no longer persecute Jesus.

Martin Luther was awestruck by seeing one of his companions

struck with lightning during a thunderstorm at Erfurt in 1502, and two weeks later was so frightened by a violent thunderstorm while returning from a visit to his family, that he decided to become a monk. So it was with Paul. But there is nothing said by Paul about a thunderstorm. What he says is that he saw a great light and heard a voice. Others have thought it must have been some kind of hallucination. Paul did not see any one nor hear any voice. He only thought he had. But none of the conditions favorable to hallucination was present in this case. If Saul had been praying and hoping and longing for a vision of Jesus, he might conceivably have imagined in some way that he had really seen Jesus. But Saul was not hoping or expecting to see Jesus. On the contrary, he believed that Jesus was an impostor, a long time dead and buried. Others have said that possibly it was a dream or vision. Saul was changed and converted by having a vision or dream of Christ. In one of his accounts of what happened he does speak of it as a vision, and how he was not disobedient unto the heavenly vision. But in his story of what happened here it is clear that if he speaks of it as a vision he does not mean the same kind of experience he had when he says he will speak of visions, and how he knew a man who was caught up into paradise, whether in the body or out of the body, he knew not. Here Paul was in the body and knew that he was in the body. He had seen a great glory and heard a great voice.

Is it possible then, that Paul was a fraud and an impostor? To further their ends and build up their schemes and institutions, men have pretended that they had some extraordinary and supernatural visitation or experience or message. History abounds in such frauds. Can it be that Paul invented the story of this Damascus experience? But to invent such a tale he must have had a reason. What could have been the reason in the case of Paul? Since there were with Saul on this memorable trip to Damascus many others, and as hostile to Christ as their leader, it is difficult to see how he could have carried through the deception. There were too many who knew the real facts. But even if it had been possible to foist upon the people some tale of an appearance of Jesus, what motive could Paul have had for so doing? Men have lied and deceived other men, but always for the sake of some thing in this present world. But what did Paul get out of his story of the appearance of Christ to him? Nothing but hatred and isolation and persecution from his own people, the Jews, and from the world at large, loneliness, danger, violence, sickness, shipwreck, bonds, imprisonment and death. For such prizes men do not commit frauds. If he invented this tale, Paul was one of the greatest impostors of all time. But who can believe that the greater part of the New Testament came from the pen of a fraud, or that the moral grandeur of character which is revealed in Paul in the pages of the Acts and the Epistles could have come from a colossal impostor?

A FACT, NOT A FRAUD

We are certain, then, that the conversion of Saul was fact and not a fraud, and that it was a fact which cannot be accounted for by sunstroke, thunderstorm, dream, vision, or hallucination. Is it possible that his conversion was the result of the working of his own conscience? Some have thought that this was the case, and they point to the words which Jesus addressed to Saul: "It is vain for thee to kick against the pricks." The "pricks," they think, must have been the pricks of conscience. They picture for us a Saul whose conscience has been condemning him for the persecution of the Christians. The angel look on the face of Stephen as he was stoned to death, the beautiful prayer he made as he was dying for those who stoned him, the patience and resignation and forgiveness which Saul had noted in those whom he had arrested and persecuted for worshiping Christ, all this, we are told, was beginning to ferment in his conscience, and what happened on the road to Damascus was a great victory of conscience. It was Saul's surrender to the voice of God in his heart. But not only is there not the slightest evidence to show that Saul's conscience was troubling him, but we have his own explicit statement, made long after, that he had no misgivings as to the rectitude of the course he was pursuing: "I did it ignorantly in unbelief." "I verily thought with myself that I ought to do many things contrary to the name of Jesus of Nazareth." The expression, "It is hard for thee to kick against the pricks," was an ancient proverb, common to the Jews as well as to the Greeks, and it was a metaphor taken from agriculture, meaning that it is vain for the oxen to kick against the goad of the driver. So Saul in persecuting the Church was fighting against God. He was embarked on an enterprise in which he was doomed to failure.

There is one thing only which is sufficient to explain the sudden overturning in Saul's life, and that is the explanation which Saul himself repeatedly gave, namely that Jesus Christ appeared unto him. "The God of our fathers," said Ananias when he ministered unto him, "hath appointed thee to see the Righteous One." In his testimony to the resurrection of Christ, Paul mentions this appearance of Christ to him on the way to Damascus as of equal significance with the appearance of Jesus to Peter, to the twelve, to the five hundred brethren, to James. "And last of all, he was seen of me also, as of one born out of due time. For I am the least of the apostles, that am not meet to be called an apostle, because I persecuted the Church of God. But by the grace of God I am what I am."

What Paul meant when he wrote those words was that there was nothing in his past history or his own character or desires or ambitions which accounted for his becoming an apostle of Jesus Christ. This sudden and overwhelming change in his life, which turned the cruel blasphemer into the slave and prisoner of Christ, was due to one thing: Jesus appeared unto him. It was a surpassing act of God's grace and mercy. It was so wondrous an exhibition of God's power and grace that Paul refers to his conversion as an example to all future ages of the mercy of God and of what the grace of God can accomplish in a man's heart: "For this cause I obtained mercy, that in me first—more than any other sinner—Jesus Christ might show forth all long-suffering, for a pattern to them which should hereafter believe on him to life everlasting." In the conversion of Saul of Tarsus Christianity secured its finest example of Christian living, its most logical and most powerful thinker, its most successful missionary and church builder; but above all else, in the sudden conversion of the chief of sinners, a mighty witness to the resurrection of Christ from the dead. If the chief proof of the Christian religion is the resurrection of Jesus, the chief witness to the fact of that resurrection is St. Paul. Saul became Paul, thereby proving that with God nothing shall be impossible. Because Saul became Paul we can understand the conquests of Christianity in the past ages and we can have confidence that all the great things which are promised through Jesus Christ will surely be fulfilled.

4

TEN YEARS OF WAITING

Judas and Ananias, the two men who first ministered to the blinded and stricken Saul at Damascus, have done much to redeem their names from that obloquy and odium which the betrayer of Christ and the man who lied to the Holy Ghost brought upon them. Somewhere in that long, and still existent, street called Straight, Saul spent three days in the house of Judas, without meat or drink. Even the ordinary emotional and mental strains which men experience drive from them all thought of food. How much more so such an experience as that of Saul. The whole fabric of a righteousness attained by the keeping of the law, carefully and sincerely built up with so much zeal and ardor and labor, and upon which he had based all his hopes, had suddenly collapsed at his feet before the sound of the voice of Jesus of Nazareth.

It was during these three days of silence and meditation that Saul had an opportunity to understand how complete was the failure of all that he had been undertaking. He had been seeking for righteousness and the peace that goes with it by the works of the law, and he had shown his zeal for the works of the law by persecuting the Church of Christ. The net result was blindness, weakness, condemnation, humiliation. The proud persecutor who had come to Damascus to harrass the Church lies blind and silent in the house of a charitable friend. He had submitted himself to the will of Christ when he asked Him, "What wilt thou have me to do?" and that there was some great work for him to do, Christ had intimated when He told him to go into the city and there learn what he was to do. Men who have been suddenly stricken in their sinful course and arrested by the hand of God have passed through a period of fear and self-reproach and expectation of judgment. We wonder if Saul had a similar experience. Did he who now knew himself to be the "chief of sinners" think himself too great a sinner to be saved? If so, it was not strange. But He who has commenced a good work in Saul is soon to finish it.

In a vision Christ appeared to one of the Damascan disciples and said to him, "Arise and go into the street which is called Straight, and inquire in the house of Judas for one called Saul, for behold he prayeth, and hath seen in a vision a man named Ananias coming in, and putting his hand on him, that he might receive his sight." Ananias was astonished to receive such a commission and reluctant to carry it out. The name Saul to a Christian disciple spelled danger and persecution and suffering and death. Ananias drew back from such a task, saying, "I have heard by many of this man, how much evil he hath done to the saints at Jerusalem; and here he hath authority from the chief priests to bind all that call on thy name." But the Lord answered, "Go thy way for he is a chosen vessel unto me, to bear my name before the Gentiles and kings, and the children of Israel. For I will show him how great things he must suffer for my name's sake." No longer doubting, Ananias arose and went to the house of Judas in the street called Straight. When he was admitted and was brought into the presence of Saul, he put his hands upon him and said, "Brother Saul, receive thy sight." At once the scales fell from the eyes of Saul, and his sight came back to him. That moment, forever memorable both for its physical and spiritual change, could never be forgotten by Saul.

In a brief but pathetic sentence Paul records the recovery of his sight, "And the same hour I looked upon him." The first face Saul saw in his new life was the kind, forgiving face of a Christian disciple who was willing to call him Brother. That name, "Brother," has been somewhat soiled by the usage and misusage of the centuries, and much of its original beauty and fragrance has fled. But how beautiful it appears, and how lovely it sounds, when spoken here in the house of Judas to the converted and blinded persecutor!

When he had restored sight to Saul, Ananias proceeded to

deliver to him his great commission, saying to him, "The God of our fathers hath chosen thee, that thou shouldest know his will, and see that Just One, and shouldest hear the voice of his mouth, for thou shalt be his witness unto all men of what thou hast seen and heard. And now why tarriest thou? Arise, and be baptized, and wash away thy sins, calling on the name of the Lord." Saul did not tarry. He knew that this was his acceptable time, and then and there Ananias baptized Saul of Tarsus into the Name of the Father, the Son, and the Holy Ghost. And there was joy in heaven over one sinner that repented.

THE PRAYER OF PAUL

Ananias is one of those noble men who help promote other men, themselves somewhat in the shadow. His work was well done, and when we think of what Saul has done for the kingdom of Jesus Christ, we must ever pay our tribute to that humble man who takes Saul by the hand and leads him into the Church. His act was one of great courage, great obedience, great faith and great love. Paul's prayers were the test of sincerity. Behold he prayeth! God is ever nigh the man who prays. As James Montgomery says in his matchless hymn on prayer:

> Prayer is the contrite sinner's voice
> Returning from his ways,
> While angels in their songs rejoice,
> And cry, "Behold, he prays."

Saul has seen Jesus and has received the Holy Ghost; but he is not yet ready for his great work among the Gentiles. Man is ever impatient and would hurry great events, but God is never in a hurry. Ten years are to elapse before Saul embarks upon his great task of preaching the Gospel to the heathen. Immediately upon his conversion Paul says he conferred not with flesh and blood but went into Arabia.[1] In solitude and aloofness from the world Paul was to instruct his life and lay the foundations for his mighty

---

1. I follow the order of events as Paul relates them in Galatians, and assume that the preaching at Damascus and Jerusalem mentioned in Acts 9 was after he had returned from his three years' stay in Arabia.

ministry. F. W. H. Meyer's poem "St. Paul," perhaps the finest tribute in verse ever paid to the Apostle, makes Paul say of this period in his life:

> Let no man think that sudden in a minute
> All is accomplished and the work is done:—
> Though with thine earliest dawn thou shouldst begin it,
> Scarce were it ended in thy setting sun.

> Oh the regret, the struggle and the failing!
> Oh the days desolate and useless years!
> Vows in the night, so fierce and unavailing!
> Stings of my shame and passion of my tears!

> How have I seen in Araby Orion,
> Seen without seeing, till he set again,
> Known the night-noise and thunder of the lion,
> Silence and sounds of the prodigious plain!

> How have I knelt with arms of my aspiring
> Lifted all night in irresponsive air!
> Dazed and amazed with overmuch desiring,
> Blank with the utter agony of prayer!

A part of Arabia, as the name was then used, was not far from Damascus; but many think that Paul means Arabia far to the south, the Sinaitic peninsula, where the children of Israel wandered, where the manna fell, where the Mount smoked and the earth quaked as God gave the Law to Moses, and where in later years Elijah wandered. De Quincey has a line sentence in one of his essays to the effect that no man, who does not at least salt his life with solitude, will ever unfold the capacities that are in him. Moses was forty years in the wilderness before, one day, the bush began to burn and God sent him forth to emancipate His people. John the Baptist was in the wilderness until the day of his showing unto Israel. Saint Augustine, after his wonderful conversion at Milan, second only to that of Paul himself, retired into seclusion at Tagaste; and Jesus Himself, before He commenced His ministry, was alone in the desert.

ALONE TO ARABIA

Now we follow Paul into the desert. What he encountered

there, and what he thought and did there, we are not told. But we know it was a conference, not with flesh and blood, but with God, and that when he comes forth from the desert he is equipped with the great message which he is to give to the world. It was a message, he declares, "which I neither received of any man, neither was I taught it, but by the revelation of Jesus Christ."

Returning to Damascus, Paul went straightway into the synagogues and proclaimed Jesus, that He is the Son of God. That in itself was an act of high moral courage. He might easily have chosen some other city, where the animosity toward him would not have been so great; but it was in Damascus, the city where he was commissioned to arrest and torture men who believed that Jesus was the Son of God, that Paul first proclaimed that truth. Everyone that heard him was amazed, and said, "Is not this he who destroyed them that called on this name in Jerusalem?"

What followed was not strange. Realizing the influence and power of such a witness to Christ, the very arch-persecutor now saying that he was the Messiah, the Jews plotted to take his life. When Ananias restored Saul's sight and baptized him, he told him that he had been sent to show him how many things he must suffer for the sake of the name of Christ. Now, therefore, commences that long chapter of suffering for the sake of the name of Christ, the first of those marks of the Lord Jesus which Paul was to carry in his body as certificate of his sincerity and apostleship.

PAUL AND PETER

While all the gates of the city were being guarded and the houses searched, Paul's friends lowered him from the wall of the town in a basket, in much the same manner that Rahab the harlot lowered with a cord the spies at Jericho. From Damascus Paul made his way to Jerusalem, a center of even greater danger for him. There he spent fifteen days with the leader of the apostles, Peter. Fifteen wonderful days they must have been. Paul repeatedly declares that he learned nothing of his gospel from man or other apostle. But there is no reason to believe that Peter did not tell him much of the history of the earthly life of Christ, and repeated many of the sayings of Christ, such a saying as that now so dear to the Church, which, but for Paul, would have been lost, how it is more blessed to give than to receive. Peter must have told him of the Mount of Transfiguration, and the miracles, and the agony of Gethsemane, and the Crucifixion, and the Resurrection, and the Ascension, and the descent of the Holy Spirit.

A wonderful fifteen days those must have been. But sad days too; sad, because of the memories which the familiar scenes must have awakened in the mind of Paul. Perhaps he went down to the place outside the wall of the city where he had kept the garments of those who stoned Stephen, and there recalled the angel-look on the face of Stephen, and thought of his dying prayer, "Lord Jesus, lay not this sin to their charge." It was the opinion of another brand miraculously snatched from the burning, the great Augustine, that the conversion of Saul of Tarsus was an answer to the dying prayer of Stephen. Familiar streets and houses would remind Saul of his mad persecuting days and bring the poignant stab of penitential remorse to his heart.

> "Saint," did I say? with your remembered faces,
> Dear men and women, whom I sought and slew!
> Ah, when we mingle in the heavenly places
> How will I weep to Stephen and to you!
>
> Oh for the strain that rang to our reviling
> Still, when the bruised limbs sank upon the sod,
> Oh for the eyes that looked their last in smiling,
> Last on this world here, but their first on God!

From the Christians generally in Jerusalem Paul met with a cool reception. That was not strange. When he tried to join himself to them, they were afraid of him and believed not that he was a disciple. They recalled his persecuting days and thought his pretended conversion was a new ruse by which he sought to trap the Christians. The pain and mortification of this must have been intense, yet Paul received it as the just recompense of his deeds. At this critical juncture emerges another of those characters who helped to give Paul to the world. Barnabas was a Cypriot, that is, from Cyprus, and Cyprus was not far from Paul's native city, Tarsus. This noble man, not misnamed Barnabas, son of Consolation, had become a disciple, and sold his land that he might contribute to the common fund. He now came forward and told the apostles of the conversion of Saul, and how he had preached boldly at Damascus. With the influential Barnabas to vouch for him, Paul went forward with his preaching and proclaimed the name of Christ in the same power in which he had once reviled it.

But what happened at Damascus now happened at Jerusalem. The Jews plotted to kill him. If Paul had any doubt as to the course he ought to pursue, this was made clear to him by a vision he had when praying in the temple. He says that the Lord appeared unto him saying, "Make haste and get thee quickly out of Jerusalem, for they will not receive thy testimony concerning me." Paul's answer shows how he acknowledged the impossibility of his present situation, and the unlikelihood of his securing a hearing from the Jews, for he says, "Lord, they know that I imprisoned and beat in every synagogue them that believed on thee, and when the blood of thy martyr Stephen was shed, I also was standing by, and consenting unto his death, and kept the raiment of them that slew him." It must have been with a feeling of sadness that Paul saw his first effort at preaching end in failure and, consenting to the entreaties of his friends at Jerusalem, let them conduct him to the seacoast at Caesarea, where he took ship for his native city of Tarsus.

INTERLUDE IN TARSUS

What Paul did during the seven years at Tarsus we are not told. It is quite possible that during these years he won for Christ some of those kinsmen to whom afterwards he sends his greetings at Rome, and perhaps, also, his sister, the playmate of his childhood days, and his sister's son, who afterwards saved his life at Jerusalem. Perhaps he took advantage of this period of retirement and waiting to acquaint himself with the thought and philosophy of the pagan world, for Tarsus was one of the chief centers of Greek learning and philosophy. To this period of preparation at Tarsus is to be assigned a remarkable experience, concerning which Paul says that whether in the body or out of it, he knew not, he was caught up into Paradise and heard unspeakable words, which it is not lawful for man to utter. In connection with this ecstatic experience, Paul mentions his "thorn in the flesh" and it may be that this mysterious malady dates from this period of waiting at Tarsus.

While Paul was in retirement at Tarsus, and, to outward vision, a failure, a great event, momentous for the destiny of the world, had taken place. Under the guidance of the Holy Spirit, Peter had preached the Gospel to the noble Roman centurion, Cornelius, at Caesarea, who became the first fruits of the Gentile world. This was an event of tremendous significance, for it meant that the Gospel had burst the bond of its narrow Judaistic childhood and had started upon its course as a world-conquering faith. The conversion of Cornelius was soon followed by the conversion of a great number of Greeks at Antioch. Some of the disciples who had been driven out of Jerusalem had gone as far as the Island of Cyprus and to Antioch, where they preached the Gospel first of all to the Jews and afterwards to the Greeks also. News of this preaching came to the Church at Jerusalem, and Barnabas, who himself was a Greek-speaking Jew, and a native of Cyprus, and in all probability well acquainted with Antioch, was sent down to take charge of the work at Antioch. When he arrived upon the scene, he at once recognized the great importance of what was taking place, and feeling the need of a helper, one who could meet the situation better than he could himself, he went down to Tarsus, where he found Paul and brought him back with him to Antioch. There the two men labored for a whole year. Paul at length had found his place.

At the time of Paul Antioch was one of the three great cities of the world, the other two being Rome and Alexandria. It was situated on the Orontes River, sixteen miles from the coast, and not far from the Taurus and Lebanon ranges of mountains. Its situation was strategic, for to its gates came the commerce of the Mediterranean, and that of the great caravan routes to Mesopotamia. The city was founded about the year 300 B.C. by Seleucus, one of the generals among whom Alexander divided his Empire. It soon became great in wealth and in population. When the Roman Province of Syria was created, Antioch became its capital. The city was one of architectural grandeur and splendor. A great Corso, or boulevard, ran the entire length of it, and gigantic walls, sections of which are still standing, encircled it. It abounded in temples, stadia, parks and palaces. The population was a mixed multitude

of Greeks and Orientals. It was a center and gathering-place for
astrologers, jugglers, impostors, charlatans and magicians.

Near the city was the grove of Daphne, where stood the great
temple to Apollo, the god of Light, at whose impetuous pursuit
Daphne had been changed into a wreath of laurel. Here in the
deep recesses of this scented and well-watered grove, the devotees
of the god of Light pursued by day and night the shameful works
of darkness. Upon the great crag of Mount Silpius, there had been
carved the likeness of Charon, the ferryman of Death's River, and
this dark face "looked down upon a scene of vice, licentiousness,
luxury and splendor, such as the world has seldom witnessed."
Such was Antioch, the cradle of Gentile Christianity, the place
from which the first world missionaries departed and where the
disciples were first called "Christians." Little did the vulgar rabble
of the street of Antioch, or the scented and perfumed debauchees
of the groves of Daphne, when they spoke the word "Christian" in
derision or quiet contempt and scorn, imagine that after Antioch
with all its temples and palaces and groves and idols had become a
heap of ruins, the city would be remembered chiefly because there
the followers of Jesus were first called "Christians," and because
Paul and Barnabas set out to preach the Gospel to the world from
this city.

5

THE UTTERMOST PARTS

It is a March morning in the year 45. The harbor at Seleucia, the port of Antioch, at the mouth of the Orontes River, is filled with shipping from all parts of the world. Large grain ships from Alexandria lie close to the wharves, unloading their golden treasure, and taking on board the goods which have come down from Mesopotamia through the mountain passes to Antioch. An eight-oared barge with an awning raised above it is being rowed rapidly out to a fleet of triremes which has just anchored in the bay, and the Roman Governor of Syria is going on board to pay his respects to the Admiral of the fleet. The docks and wharves are the scene of the greatest confusion and animation and excitement as the ships come in or prepare to depart.

In this mixed multitude at the waterfront, our attention is centered upon a little group kneeling on the stones of the pier next to a vessel, the sails of which are thrashing in the brisk morning wind, and which is about to sail to Cyprus. After they have prayed for a few minutes, they rise from their knees, and three men bid an affectionate farewell to their friends who have come down to see them off, and then board the ship for Cyprus. The words of command are spoken, the anchor is hoisted, the rudder shifted, and the wind filling the great sails, carries the ship rapidly out of the harbor into the open sea where it heads for Cyprus, the dim outline of which can barely be discerned from the deck of the vessel. None of the loungers on the docks at Seleucia, none of the merchants and traders, and none of the sea-captains or Roman naval officers, seeing that little vessel parting the waves with its prow as it started for Cyprus, paid the slightest attention to it or to the three men who stood on the deck waving a farewell to their friends on shore.

Yet it was the beginning of the most memorable voyage in the history of mankind. Compared with this voyage, the results and consequences of the voyages of Columbus, Vasco da Gama, Magellan and the Vikings were of little moment, for this was the commencement of the Christian Odyssey. Christ had told His disciples before His ascension that they were to be His witnesses in Judea, in Samaria, and in the uttermost parts of the earth. The Gospel has been preached in Judea and in Samaria; now it is to be proclaimed in the uttermost parts of the earth. More than any ship that ever cleft the waves with its prow, that frail craft bound for the shores of Cyprus carried with it a man and an idea which are to affect the destinies of the human race.

This memorable voyage was the natural fulfillment of Paul's original commission, that he was to preach the Gospel to the Gentiles. But it was not undertaken without a special demonstration of the Holy Spirit. While godly men in the Church at Antioch kept a day of prayer and fasting, the Holy Spirit, in those ways which for Him are ever possible, directed the believers in Antioch to separate unto Him for a special work Barnabas and Paul. This they did by prayer and the laying on of hands. Thus ordained to their great and holy task, Barnabas and Paul left Antioch for Seleucia, where they took a ship for Cyprus. Cyprus was a natural place for them to stop first on their journey, for it was the home of Barnabas, and already the seeds of the Gospel had been sown there by some of the refugees who had been driven out of Jerusalem at the time of the persecution which arose after the stoning of Stephen.

MEET MARK

Accompanying the two missionaries was a young man, Mark. He was not ordained and set apart for the particular task of a missionary, but seems to have gone along as a relative, perhaps an attendant, of Barnabas, who was his uncle. This Mark was the son of Mary, who owned a large house in Jerusalem, and in which the disciples were accustomed to worship. It was in her house that they had met together for prayer when Peter was delivered out of the prison of Herod. He is supposed to be the author of the Gospel which bears his name, and he has commonly been identified with that certain young man who followed Christ into the garden of Gethsemane, and fled naked, leaving his linen cloth behind him, when Christ was arrested.

In a few hours the ship made the port of Salamis on the eastern end of the island of Cyprus. This Salamis is not to be confused with the island and bay of Salamis near Athens, where in the year 480 B.C. the Greek fleet under Themistocles defeated the Persian fleet of Xerxes. Yet at this Salamis, in Cyprus, there was also a land and naval battle between the forces of Artaxerxes, the son and successor to Xerxes, and the Greek army and navy. Cyprus was the ancient home of the Kittim, the descendants of Javan, one of the grandsons of Noah. It is recorded in Genesis that the isles of the Gentiles were divided among the sons of Javan. The island of Cyprus is 110 miles in length by 30 to 50 miles in breadth. It is very mountainous and was long noted in the ancient world for the richness of its copper mines. At the time Paul landed on the island it was a province of the Roman Empire, under the rule of a pro-consul, and there were many Jews in the island.

After preaching for some time in the synagogue at Salamis, Paul and his companions passed through the island, until they came to the city of Paphos, situated at the western end. Here was the seat of the Roman government, also the center of the worship of Venus. The Roman Governor, or pro-consul, Sergius Paulus, described as a "prudent man," heard of the preaching of Barnabas and Paul and gave them an invitation to declare to him the word of God. He was evidently greatly impressed by what he heard, and was inclined to accept the Gospel and believe in Christ.

ENTER ELYMAS

But attached to his court was a false prophet, or sorcerer, a degenerate Jew whose name was Elymas. The sorcerer was a most important personage in that ancient world. He combined the offices of scientist, physician, astrologer and fortune-teller.

With the decline of the old Roman faith, superstition gained a new dominion over the hearts of men, and in every great center of the Roman world there was a swarm of astrologers, magicians, mountebanks, impostors and all that tribe who pretend to explore the occult world. This sorcerer Elymas saw that he would lose his place at the court if his master, the pro-consul, accepted the Gospel. He, therefore, withstood the apostles, seeking to turn away the pro-consul from the faith. From the great indignation of Paul, we judge that the sorcerer bitterly attacked the apostles and blasphemed the name of Christ. Everywhere in the Scriptures the sin of turning men away from the truth, or keeping them from faith in God and in Christ, is represented in the darkest colors. It is not strange that a speedy and striking judgment is pronounced upon this blasphemer who would have kept the Roman deputy from believing in Christ. Fastening his eyes upon him, Paul said, as he alone could say it, "O full of all subtilty and all mischief, thou child of the devil, thou enemy of all righteousness, wilt thou not cease to pervert the right ways of the Lord? And now, behold, the hand of the Lord is upon thee, and thou shalt be blind, not seeing the sun for a season." Immediately there fell upon Elymas a mist and a darkness, and he went about seeking someone to lead him by the hand.

The pro-consul, seeing this miracle of judgment, was the more convinced that the Gospel was true, and confessed his faith in Christ. It is in connection with this incident that Saul is first called Paul, and many have thought that the name was taken by him in honor of his first notable convert from the Gentile world, Sergius Paulus. This miracle, and the conversion of the Roman pro-consul, concluded the work of Paul and Barnabas in the island of Cyprus. They sailed from the harbor of Paphos, and after a brief journey landed at Perga on the coast of Pamphylia. Here John Mark departed from them and returned to Jerusalem. Just what his motives were we are not told; but Paul evidently regarded them as unworthy, for we learn that he was greatly incensed at the departure of John Mark. Various reasons have been assigned for the return of Mark—that he was jealous of the leadership and influence of Paul, to whom Barnabas now takes the secondary place—that he was homesick for his mother and his friends, and, most probable of all, that he was frightened at the dangers which would confront them as they proceeded from the coast into the robber-infested mountain country of the interior.

Paul did no preaching at Perga. The country about Perga is low and malarial, and in the summer season the population withdraws to the mountains. Paul probably traveled northward with one of these migrating bands. In his Letter to the Galatians, the people who lived in the high mountain country to which he traveled after leaving Perga, he afterwards wrote, "Ye know that because of an infirmity of the flesh I preached the Gospel unto you the first time." It has therefore been supposed that Paul was taken sick at Perga with an attack of malaria and that this sickness was the occasion of his leaving the great trade routes and setting out over the mountains into the dangerous country of the interior. Here Paul commenced his experiences, those "perils of robbers" and "perils of waters" and "perils of the wilderness," of which he afterwards speaks, and of which he was to know so much before his journeys were over. These mountains of Asia Minor which Paul and Barnabas traversed are described by those who have visited them as picturesque and beautiful in their rugged grandeur; but Paul gives us no record of his impressions. His mind was set upon the great task of preaching the Gospel, and his heart was filled with wonder at the exceeding riches of God's grace, rather than at the loveliness of nature.

In the Synagogue on the Sabbath

After a week's journey, the two apostles reached Antioch of Pisidia, a town of great commercial importance. Paul was now in the Roman Province of Galatia. When the Sabbath day came, they went into the Synagogue and sat down. The fact that they sat down upon entering was sufficient to let the elders of the Synagogue know that the strangers were persons accustomed to teach or to preach. The Synagogue was the cradle of the Christian Church. Its order of worship became the custom of the church service and in the Synagogue was heard the first proclamation of the gospel of redeeming love. If we had entered that Synagogue of Antioch on the Sabbath of long ago, we would have seen on one side the lattice-work partition behind which were the veiled and silent women. At one end of the plain room, undecorated by sculpture of any sort, was the reading desk, and near it, facing the rest of the congregation, the "chief seats" of which Christ said the Pharisees were so fond. After the prayers and the reading of the Law and the Prophets, the rulers of the Synagogue, noting the strangers in their midst, said to them in all courtesy, "Ye men and brethren, if ye have any word of exhortation for the people, say on." It was Paul, and not Barnabas, who accepted the invitation.

Rising to his feet, and beckoning with his hand, his characteristic opening gesture, Paul said, "Men of Israel, and ye that fear God, give audience." This introduction would seem to indicate that Paul was speaking not only to Jews, but to God-fearing Gentiles who were present in the Synagogue.

The sermon which Paul preached that Sabbath in Antioch, his first recorded sermon, was characteristic of his manner and style of preaching on all occasions. He commenced with Old Testament history and told the story of Israel as the unfolding of the divine purpose in the preparation of the world for the coming of Christ and the proclamation of the truth. This he followed by a brief recital of the great facts of Christ's life and death and resurrection. Through this Jesus, whom God raised from the dead, and who saw no corruption, there was to be preached unto men the forgiveness of sin. All who believed in Him would be justified of all their sins. The sermon closed with an earnest warning and admonition that those who heard the words of the Gospel would not despise the message or mock at it.

INVITED TO PREACH AGAIN

The preacher's evident familiarity with Old Testament history, and his burning zeal and ardor, made a deep impression on his auditors, especially upon the Gentiles who were present, and who, when the congregation had broken up, besought Paul that he would preach to them again the next Sabbath. The formal preaching in the Synagogue was followed by earnest conversation between the Jews and the religious proselytes and Paul and Barnabas, who encouraged them in their interest and persuaded them to continue in the grace of God. The result was that the next Sabbath day almost the whole city crowded in and around the Synagogue to hear these eloquent speakers. But the presence and the deep interest of so many of the Gentiles aroused the envy and resentment of the Jews, who, up to this time, had heard Paul's message without any irritation. Now they contradicted him and blasphemed the Name in which he was preaching.

Aroused by this opposition, Paul and Barnabas boldly declare to the Jews that they have fulfilled a solemn duty in preaching the Gospel first of all to them, but, now that they have rejected the Gospel and judged themselves unworthy of everlasting life, they will turn to the Gentiles. In so doing they say that they will be fulfilling the commandments of the Lord, who has set them to be a light to the Gentiles and for salvation unto the ends of the earth. That company of Jews who rejected the Gospel were the first of a vast multitude, increasing in number from age to age, made up of all kindreds and tribes and nations and tongues, who, in the sad and tragic words of the Apostle, "judged themselves unworthy of everlasting life." How many by their open and scornful rejection, or by their foolish procrastination and indifference, have so passed judgment upon themselves.

The Gentiles heard this message that henceforth the Gospel was to be for them, with great joy, and glorified the words of the Lord; but the Jews were filled with envy and anger and stirred up not only the chief men of the city, but the devout and honorable women, who raised a persecution against Paul and Barnabas and compelled them to depart out of the city. When they had shaken off the dust of their feet, as Christ had told the disciples to do, whenever a city rejected their message, as a testimony against the city, Paul and Barnabas departed and went unto Iconium, some ninety-three miles to the southeast. Luke, who tells this story, says of the Gentiles, and it was true of many of the Jews who believed, that "as many as were ordained to eternal life believed." Here, then, in this first missionary journey, in the proclamation of the Gospel to the heathen of Galatia, we are confronted by the great mystery of predestination. If this doctrine raises difficulty, let it be remembered that if it be left out there are still greater difficulties to face. Luke states it, not in any controversial or theological way, but as an historical fact, as the natural result of the preaching of the Gospel by Paul and Barnabas at Antioch, that "as many as believed"—no more or no less— "were ordained unto eternal life." Why do some men receive and obey the Gospel, and others, with the same environment and background and training, reject it? The answer of St. Luke is that "as many as had been ordained unto eternal life believed."

At Iconium Paul and Barnabas repeated their success at Antioch, and great multitudes of Jews and Greeks believed. But the unbelieving Jews stirred up the Gentile population so that there was a division of opinion in the city concerning the two visitors. Part held with the Jews and part with the apostles. Those who were hostile to the apostles gathered a mob and rushed toward the dwelling-place of Paul and Barnabas, intending to stone them. But they got word of the impending assault and fled out of the city into Lystra, still further to the southeast. At Iconium, as elsewhere, the plot and persecution were the result of the hostility of the Jews.

The Book of Acts tells us little about Paul's long stay at Iconium. But where history is silent, legend has been busy, and a popular romance of the second century, called "The Acts of Paul and Thecla," gives many alleged incidents of Paul's visit to Iconium. Thecla was a young woman of one of the chief families of Iconium, and hearing from a window the preaching of Paul, was greatly impressed and determined to become a Christian. She was engaged to a young man named Thamyris, but because of the effect of the Apostle's words, she broke off her engagement, intending to devote her life as a virgin to Christ. Her relatives and that of the young man blamed Paul for this interference with family life, and scourged him and drove him out of the city, and Thecla herself was condemned to be burned alive. She was fastened to the stake and the flames were already leaping up when the rain fell and extinguished the fire. Escaping from her adversaries, Thecla followed Paul to Antioch, where she was persecuted again, but rescued by Tryphaena, a woman of wealth and influence. It is quite possible that there is a degree of fact in this romance of the second century.

A PICTURE OF PAUL

It is in this romance, "The Acts of Paul and Thecla," that we have one of the earliest descriptions of the Apostle's personal appearance. The story describes him as a short man, bandy-legged, healthy looking, with his eyebrows meeting each other, inclined to be red-haired, of gracious presence. Renan, in his Life of Paul, speaks of him as an "ugly little Jew." Others have guessed that Paul was little on the ground that the people of Lystra took him for the god Mercury, who was not of great stature, though, as we shall see, that was not the reason why the people of Lystra thought that Paul was Mercury, but because he was the chief speaker. The idea that Paul had a weak personal appearance is based largely upon what his enemies at Corinth said, that though his letters were weighty and powerful his bodily presence was weak. Many have conjectured that Paul's thorn in the flesh was a disease of the eyes, and that this detracted from the power and influence of his presence. But the way in which Paul fastened his eyes on the sorcerer, Elymas, at Paphos, and on the cripple at Lystra, and the way in which he looked steadfastly on the council at Jerusalem, does not indicate that there was anything weak about the glance of his eyes. The fact is, we know nothing about Paul's personal appearance. Yet we can be sure that the tabernacle of so great and burning a spirit could not have been without a degree of grace and nobility. It is the soul, after all, that makes the body powerful and commanding.

A MINISTRY IN LYSTRA

In fleeing from one city to another, the apostles were undoubtedly mindful of the words of Jesus when He sent forth the twelve disciples, "When they persecute you in this city, flee ye into another. "The city to which they now fled, Lystra, was in a new region called Lycaonia, which means " The Land of the Wolf." The country was well named, for it was wild and barbarous and the seat of pagan worship. Here we have no record of Paul preaching in a synagogue, and therefore, the work at Lystra may be considered as the first preaching to a purely Gentile population. It may be that Paul felt the need of a special sign at Lystra to commend the Gospel and its messenger to the heathen population. At all events, he commenced his work by a great miracle. By the roadside there sat a poor cripple who, from his mother's womb, had never walked. This cripple had listened to the preaching of the Gospel, and Paul, beholding him and observing that he had faith to be healed, said to him with a loud voice, "Stand upright on thy feet." At the word, the man leaped up and walked. This miracle, and the words which Paul addressed to the cripple, remind us of the healing by Peter of the lame man at the Gate Beautiful of the Temple. When the people saw what Paul had done, they cried out, using the provincial language of Lycaonia, "The gods are come down to us in the likeness of men." That the gods came down occasionally to visit the earth and walked with men was no strange idea to the pagans. On this occasion they even went so far as to identify the supposed deities, calling Barnabas Jupiter, and Paul Mercury, because he was the "chief speaker." In the mythology of ancient Greece Jupiter was often accompanied by Mercury on earthly rambles.

The comments of the people upon the miracle which they had seen, and how they took Barnabas and Paul to be Jupiter and Mercury, was made in the Lycaonian tongue, which Paul and Barnabas did not understand; and they had no inkling of what the people had said, or what they meant, until the priest of Jupiter appeared before them at the gate of the city, bringing oxen and garlands. Paul and Barnabas then understood what they intended to do. Seeing that they were to be made the objects of sacrifice and worship, the apostles rent their clothes and ran in among the people crying out, "Sirs, why do ye these things? We also are men of like passions with you." This whole dramatic scene has been preserved for us in a wonderful way by Raphael's cartoon in the Sistine chapel at Rome. In that painting, one can see the oxen with the garlands and beads on their heads, and the attendant priest about to lift the knife and offer the sacrifice. The speech of the apostles, no doubt that of Paul, for it closely resembles the brief address he made to the Athenians on Mars Hill, is well worth repeating:

"Sirs, who do ye these things? we also are men of like passions with you, and preach unto you that ye should turn from these vanities unto the living God, which made heaven and earth and the sea and all things that are therein. Who in times past suffered all nations to walk in their own ways. Nevertheless, he left not himself without witness, in that he did good and gave us rain from heaven, and fruitful seasons, filling our hearts with food and gladness."

This beautiful and courageous address, calling the whole system of sacrifices "vanities," with the garlanded oxen before them, had the desired effect, and the people refrained from their contemplated act of devotion.

ENEMIES AGAIN

The next scene at Lystra was the very reverse of what we have just witnessed. The populace of Jerusalem on Palm Sunday cried, "Hosanna in the highest to the son of David!" but two days afterwards they were shouting, " Crucify Him! Crucify Him!" So was it with the apostles of Jesus at Lystra. The enemies of Paul at Antioch had followed him to Iconium, and now to Lystra, where they stirred up the populace against the apostles. Having been restrained from their act of sacrifice, and, no doubt, all too ready to believe that they had been the credulous victims of impostors, men who were impersonating Jupiter and Mercury, the fickle population turned on Paul and Barnabas and stoned them. As the chief speaker, Paul seems to have been the chief victim and object of their rage. What Saul of Tarsus had urged the people to do at Jerusalem, when they stoned Stephen, now Paul himself, as if by divine retribution, encountered. In the catalogue of his woes and suffering, Paul says, "Once I was stoned." This was the stoning at Lystra. He was dragged out of the city by the mob and left for dead. But as soon as the passions of the mob had subsided and the people had broken up and gone to their homes, a little company of faithful friends of Paul ventured out of the city in the gathering gloom, and groped among the stones and rubbish until they came upon the broken, bleeding body of the Apostle. As they stood about him, weeping and praying, Paul suddenly recovered and rose up and came with them into the city.

Among those who went out to find him and minister to him was a young Lycaonian youth, Timothy, destined to be Paul's chief friend, his child beloved in the faith. His grandmother, Lois, and his mother, Eunice, devout Jewesses, lived at Lystra, but his father was a Greek. Paul's trip to Lystra was well worth while, if it accomplished nothing more than the conversion of Timothy. At the very end of his life, in his last message to the world, Paul recalls the beginning of their friendship at Lystra amid danger and persecution, for he writes to Timothy, "Thou didst follow my persecutions and afflictions which came unto me at Lystra, but out of them all the Lord delivered me."

Weak and ill, suffering from the terrible experiences through which he had just passed, Paul went with Barnabas to Derbe, about fifty miles southeast of Iconium. Here he won another notable convert, Gaius, one of his companions on future journeys. At Derbe Paul was not far from his own native town of Tarsus, and by going through the mountain passes at the Gates of Cilicia, he could easily have reached home and safety. But he turned back courageously to face the dangers and persecutions in the cities out of which he had just been driven. Instead of going to Tarsus they returned again to Lystra, to Iconium, and to Antioch, confirming the souls of the disciples and exhorting them to continue in the faith, and telling them that through much tribulation they must enter into the Kingdom of God. In each one of these towns they established a church by ordaining elders, who were to have the oversight of the congregation.

It must have been with a great deal of prayer and tender pleading that Paul and Barnabas bade farewell to these little groups of believers in the midst of the great pagan population, commending them to the Lord in whom they had believed, and charging them to be faithful unto Him. From Antioch and Pisidia they came down to the coast at Perga where they had first landed. From Perga they went down to the seaport of Attalia, and there took ship for Antioch in Syria. After a short voyage, they sailed into the mouth of the Orontes River, disembarked at Seleucia, where they had started, and going up to Antioch, told all that God had done with them and how He had opened the door of faith unto the Gentiles. Thus ended the first great missionary journey.

6

A BATTLE FOR CONSCIENCE

One of the tests of a great man is his willingness to part company with his friends for conscience's sake. It is one thing to stand for a principle against the world and the open adversaries of the truth. It is another, and a more difficult, thing to stand for principle against one's own friends and associates. We are now to behold St. Paul in a noble exhibition of this high courage and daring. The Church at Antioch was greatly refreshed and rejoiced by the tidings of what Paul and Barnabas had accomplished on that first missionary journey and how God had opened a door of faith unto the Gentiles. But soon a cloud appeared on the horizon. The conversion of the Roman centurion, Cornelius, by Peter, and the open advocacy by Peter of the privileges of the Gentiles to hear and receive the Gospel, and the subsequent work among the Gentiles at Antioch and in the cities and countries visited by Paul and Barnabas, ought to have settled the question about the place of the Gentiles in the Church. But not so. Influential Jewish Christians from Jerusalem came down to Antioch and said to the Christians there, "Except ye be circumcised after the custom of Moses, ye cannot be saved." In short, this meant that to become a Christian one had first of all to become a Jew and to keep the law of Moses in all its detail.

The crisis was great, perhaps the greatest in the history of the Christian Church, because it arose at the very beginning of Christian history, and any decision made would affect the future history of the Church. In this critical hour, Paul appeared on the scene of events and with his clear vision and magnificent courage led the

Church to a right decision and delivered it forever from the bondage of bigotry and the worship of outward rites and practices. We must not be harsh in our judgment of the earnest Jewish Christians at Jerusalem, who were convinced that in order to be saved a man must submit to the ancient customs of Moses. We must remember that they had back of them the great traditions of a chosen people and that the Jewish rites and observances, and circumcision in particular, had been for ages the sign and seal of admission into the circle of the covenant people of God. The Jews had never shut the gate of salvation to the outside world, and many a proselyte had been brought in, but always through the gate of circumcision and submission to the Jewish customs and laws. There were many who still thought that these customs must be observed before a Gentile should be received into the Christian Church. The conflict, therefore, was not merely one for freedom and for conscience's sake, but for the truth of the Gospel and for its cardinal doctrine, that men are saved by the infinite grace of God, by faith in Jesus Christ and Him crucified, and not by works of the law.

AN INTRODUCTION TO TITUS

The discussion grew so intense at Antioch that the Church there appointed Paul and Barnabas and certain others to go up to Jerusalem and consult with the apostles and the elders on this important question. This led to what we may call the First Council of the Christian Church. Among those who went up with Paul and Barnabas to Jerusalem, was a young Greek by the name of Titus, who in his own person was the incarnation of the problem now before the Church. Titus is one of that immortal company of men who have the distinction of being known as the friends and companions of Paul. Singularly enough, he is not mentioned in the Acts, but quite frequently in the letters of Paul. It is probable that he was a native of Antioch, and since Paul calls him "my true child after a common faith," very likely converted by the preaching of Paul.

Titus was much younger than Paul, yet was assigned important duties and offices. He was with Paul during his long stay at Ephesus and was his personal messenger and ambassador to the Church at

Corinth, where grave abuses had appeared. He was appointed by Paul to superintend the organization of churches in the island of Crete, but was expecting to rejoin Paul in Nicopolis after his release from his first imprisonment. The last reference we have to Titus is in Paul's final letter during his second imprisonment at Rome, where he says that Titus has gone to Dalmatia. One of Paul's epistles is addressed to Titus, and in this letter we have stated many of the qualifications for the office of minister and elder, and a general description of what is expected of a Christian man.

A JOURNEY TO JERUSALEM

When the Council convened at Jerusalem, with James probably presiding, Peter made the first address. Certain Pharisees, who had become Christians, had insisted at Jerusalem that it was needful to circumcise the Gentiles and to charge them to keep the law of Moses. In his brief, but admirable, address, Peter gave an account of his own preaching of the Gospel to the Gentiles, referring to the conversion of Cornelius, and that the Holy Spirit had been given unto the Gentiles as well as unto the Jewish Christians. He declared that it was tempting God to put a yoke upon the neck of the disciples and that the Gentiles would be saved by the grace of God, in like manner as the Jews. This speech was followed by remarks from Barnabas and Paul, telling of their works among the Gentiles in distant lands and what wonders God had wrought. Then James gave his opinion. This James was the brother of the Lord, probably the author of the epistle which bears his name, and the recognized leader of the Church at Jerusalem. James quotes a prophecy of Amos which speaks of the restoration of the tabernacle of David and how the residue of men are to seek after the Lord, and all Gentiles upon whom the name of God is called. In short, the preaching to the Gentiles and their acceptance of the Gospel was a plain fulfillment of prophecy. His sentence, therefore, is that they do not trouble the Gentile with these old Jewish laws, but ask them to refrain from four things: idolatry, uncleanness, from things strangled and from blood. Since in every city there were Jewish synagogues where the law of Moses was read, to violate any one of these four customs would be the cause of irritation and conflict.

IDOLATRY

Two of the things mentioned by James involved great principles of conduct, idolatry and sensuality: It was the custom for the Gentile people to buy and eat the meat which had been offered on pagan altars. It is easy to see how this custom maintained by Gentile Christians would give great and needless offense to the Jewish Christian. It was a case where all things are lawful but all things are not expedient. Paul afterwards declared that an idol is nothing at all, and intimates that he would as soon eat meat that had been offered before an idol as meat that had not been so used, and that meat does not commend a man to God. But he says in a memorable sentence, that he will not use his liberty to become a stumbling block to his brethren and that if meat makes his brother to offend, he will eat no meat while the world stands. On the whole it was just as well for the Gentile Christians, even in their daily customs, clearly to be separated from that idolatry which hitherto had pervaded and permeated their whole life.

PERSONAL PURITY

The other great principle was that of personal purity. The fact that James thought it necessary to mention the subject of sensuality and fornication, shows how common this terrible vice was in the pagan world. From Paul's Letter to the Romans, where he gives a survey of pagan morality, we know that the things of which it is a shame even to speak, were the common practices of the pagan world. It is sadly true that these things still persist, for human nature still persists, but they are not done in the open as they were in that ancient day, and they have upon them today the condemnation and scorn of all right-minded men. This complete change in the idea of morality and personal conduct is one of the striking results of the preaching of the Gospel. The sin of sensuality was eating like a canker into the soul and body of ancient civilization, and this not on the testimony of Christian writers only, but on the testimony of the pagan writers themselves. Matthew Arnold tells the truth when he writes of that age, "Deep weariness and sated lust made human life a hell." The other two things mentioned, that they should refrain from eating things that had been strangled and from blood, because the Jews believed that life was in the blood, were perhaps wise provisions; but in the course of time they soon disappeared, as they dealt with the peculiarities and inconsequentialities of Jewish custom.

Paul and his party had won a complete victory. Titus himself, put forward as a concrete illustration of the problem with which they had to deal, a Gentile coming into the Church, was not compelled to be circumcised. A circular letter was drafted by the Council, and in the hands of two representatives, Judas, or Barnabas, and Silas, sent down to the churches of Antioch and Syria and Cilicia. The letter was as follows:

"For as much as we have heard, that certain which went out from us have troubled you with words, subverting your souls, to whom we gave no commandment; it seemed good unto us, having come to one accord, to choose out men and send them unto you with our beloved Barnabas and Paul, men that hazarded their lives for the name of our Lord Jesus Christ. We have sent, therefore, Judas and Silas, who themselves also shall tell you the same thing by word of mouth. For it seemed good to the Holy Ghost and to us, to lay upon you no greater burden than these necessary things; that ye abstain from things offered to idols, and from blood, and from things strangled, and from fornication, from which if ye keep yourselves, it shall be well with you. Fare ye well."

This brief letter is more precious and more important than the Magna Charta, or any bill of writing in the history of human legislation; for it is the Magna Charta of Christian freedom.

PAUL CONFRONTS PETER

So far as the formal action of the Church was concerned, the battle for freedom and deliverance from the bondage of old Jewish customs had been won. The Church had decided that to become a Christian a man does not need to become a Jew. But for the sake of this principle Paul had still to make one more noble and heroic stand, this time confronting the most illustrious of the apostles, Peter himself. When Peter came on a visit to the Church at Antioch, he fraternized freely with the Gentile Christians, as he had every reason to do, both on account of his own experience in the conversion of Cornelius, and on account of the

decision of the Church Council at Jerusalem. But it is evident that
the decision of the Church Council had not altogether removed
the feeling of resentment and jealousy in the hearts of certain
Jewish Christians, for Paul says that after "certain from James,"
that is, men who were of the extreme Jewish party at Jerusalem,
came down to Antioch, Peter no longer would eat with the Gentiles, but separated himself from them, fearing the reproach and
opposition of the Jewish party. Others followed him in this cow-
ardly and inconsistent action, and what is most surprising of all,
even Barnabas was carried away by their dissimulation. This action on the part of Peter roused Paul to righteous indignation. He
says that he "withstood him to the face," because he was to be
blamed. Confronting Peter before a group of believers at Antioch,
Paul said to him:

"If thou being a Jew livest as do the Gentiles, and not as do the
Jews, why compellest thou the Gentiles to live as do the Jews? We
being Jews by nature and not sinners of the Gentiles, yet knowing
that a man is not justified by the works of law, save through faith
in Jesus Christ, even we believed on Christ Jesus that we might be
justified by faith in Christ, and not by the works of the law:
because by the works of the law shall no flesh be justified."

In brief, Paul's telling argument was this: "Peter, by confessing
your faith in Christ, you have confessed that a man cannot be
saved by the works of the law, and you yourself have changed
from that old confidence to the ground of faith in Christ. How
then are you consistent in taking a course which would seem to
tell the Gentiles that they cannot be saved unless they submit to
those rites and customs in which you yourself no longer place a
reliance?" The scene is a painful one, and yet a magnificent
exhibition of courage. It was Peter with whom Paul had spent
the first fifteen days at Jerusalem, and it was from Peter, no
doubt, that he learned the events of the earthly life of our Lord.
Moreover, Peter was a great character in the Church and justly
celebrated for the prominence which he had taken in the earthly
ministries of his Lord. He was also a much older man than Paul.

For all these reasons it must have been painful and difficult for
Paul, the least of the apostles, as he says himself to be, one who
not only was not of the original band of the Twelve, but had
blasphemed the name of Christ, and persecuted His Church, to

rebuke and reprimand publicly the Apostle Peter. But there were at stake greater issues than personal relationships; the truth of the Gospel was more important than any bond of friendship. Peter was to be blamed, and Paul pronounced a just censure upon him. From what Paul tells us in his Letter to the Galatians, he had to rebuke Barnabas also, and this must have been harder for him to do than to rebuke Peter, for it was the noble and magnanimous Barnabas who had commended Paul to the Church when all others suspected his motives and looked upon him as a false convert, and it was through the intervention of Barnabas that Paul was introduced to his life's work at Antioch. Yet both men were to be blamed, and Paul blamed them.

In times of controversy and testimony to the truth there are always those who deprecate strife, and if they had been at Antioch when the inconsistent conduct of Peter and Barnabas aroused the indignation of Paul, would have counseled Paul, for the sake of peace and unity, to say nothing about the matter. But Paul was loyal to the truth and performed his painful duty with an eye single to the service of God. It is through the loyalty and courage of men like Paul that the truth is maintained and handed down from generation to generation. If Paul strikes us as heroic, when he encourages the panic-stricken company on the shipwrecked vessel in the Mediterranean, or when he hushes the howling mob in the streets of Jerusalem, or when he goes back to Lystra and Iconium and Antioch, just after he had been persecuted and driven out of these cities, his heroism reached a high water mark when he stood up in the assembly in the church at Antioch and rebuked Peter and Barnabas for disloyalty to their own convictions and disloyalty to the freedom of the grace of God in Jesus Christ.

Luke makes no mention of this scene in his history in the Acts of the Apostles. Perhaps he thought it was too painful. But Paul in his Letter to the Galatians tells what took place, not for the sake of self-praise, but to show how the truth must be vindicated. A wise man once said, "Faithful are the wounds of a friend and we have every reason to believe that, excitable and impulsive as Peter was by nature, he did not become angry, and received the admonition and rebuke of his brother Paul with humility and with the acknowledgment that Paul was in the right. Peter was not unac-

customed to rebukes. He had received many of them from his
Lord, and no doubt he received this one from Paul with good
grace, for the course which he had taken could not in any way be
defended. Although an apostle, truly converted and sent forth to
strengthen his brethren, Peter was not made perfect any more
than Paul. Yet this inconsistency of character in no way reflects
upon the truth of what he taught or what he wrote. According to
the old legend his consistent inconsistency pursued him down to
the very end of his ministry, for when he was fleeing from Rome
at the time of the persecution under Nero he was met on the
Appian Way by Christ. Peter said to Christ, "Whither goest thou?"
Christ answered, "I go to Rome to be crucified again." Upon this
Peter turned back to Rome and suffered martyrdom in the name
and for the sake of Christ. At the close of his second letter to the
Jews scattered throughout the world, Peter makes reference to our
"beloved brother Paul." These two men are the most interesting
personalities among those who carry the Gospel to the uttermost
parts of the earth. Long since, Peter and Paul have been reconciled, and together now in the Kingdom of the blessed they follow
the Lamb of God wherever He goes.

7

WESTWARD HO!— THE GOSPEL IN EUROPE

Paul was not content to remain long at Antioch. His heart was beyond the mountains and beyond the seas in those towns where he had preached the Gospel on the first missionary journey. Very soon, therefore, after they had come down to Antioch from the Council at Jerusalem Paul said to Barnabas, "Let us go again and visit our brethren in every city where we have preached the word of the Lord, and see how they do." Barnabas was ready to go with him; but when he proposed to take with them again his nephew, John Mark, Paul would not agree to it. His reason was that Mark had turned back when they were at Perga in Pamphylia and in the midst of the dangers of the first missionary journey. Such a man, Paul was convinced, was not fit for the responsibilities and labors of the great enterprise on which he and Barnabas were setting forth. But Barnabas, perhaps out of a better acquaintance, was persuaded of better things concerning Mark, and was determined to take him along. Thus there arose between these two great men a sharp dissension. Neither of them would yield the point, and the result was that they parted company, Barnabas taking Mark and sailing for Cyprus, and Paul taking Silas and starting across the mountains toward Galatia.

Paul has been severely censured for thus breaking with the man to whom he owed more than to any other man. It was Barnabas who had vouched for him at Jerusalem when he was under the suspicion of the disciples there, and it was Barnabas who had come to Tarsus to seek him, and had brought him to Antioch to commence the great work among the Gentiles. These feuds between Christian leaders are always sad and depressing, especially where no great moral issue is involved. Nevertheless, if Paul was convinced that Mark was not a fit companion for these journeys, it was courageous of him to refuse to take him with him, even at the cost of a break with Barnabas. In political or military crises, men should be chosen with the sole view to their capacity.

The Federal army, in the Civil War in the United States, was greatly handicapped by appointments to high command of unfit men, made by President Lincoln because of his magnanimity and friendly feeling. In the great enterprise upon which Paul was embarked, the first consideration was the ability and efficiency of those who were setting out upon it. If Paul had no confidence in Mark, it was far better that he should part company with Barnabas and go with Silas. From future references to Mark in the writings of Paul, we are glad to know that he reinstated himself in the good opinion of the great Apostle. In his Letter to Philemon Paul refers to "Mark, my fellow-worker" and in his last letter, the second to Timothy, Paul writes to Timothy, "Take Mark, and bring him with thee, for he is profitable to me for the ministry." Barnabas now fades from the apostolic picture, and our whole attention is centered upon his friend for whom he had done so much. According to an old tradition Barnabas was stoned by the Jews at Salamis on the island of Cyprus, and before dying told Mark to return and join Paul on his missionary labors. The Epistle of Barnabas, an early Christian document, one of the New Testament Apocryphal books, and thought by many to have been written by Barnabas, is a discussion of the Old Testament rites and ritual, and how they found their fulfillment in Christ and the Gospel. The letter commences with these words, "All happiness to you, my sons and daughters, in the name of our Lord Jesus Christ who loved us in peace" and ends with this message, "Wherefore I have given the more diligence to write unto you according to my ability, that ye might rejoice. Farewell, children of love and peace."

Paul's new companion, Silas, was one of those who had been sent down from the Council at Jerusalem to publish their decree concerning the Gentiles at Antioch and elsewhere. Leaving Antioch, Paul and Silas passed through the Syrian Gates to Issus, where in 333 B.C., Alexander the Great had defeated the Persians. Their route took him through Tarsus, Paul's native town, and there, no doubt, he tarried for a little, recalling the scenes of his childhood, and perhaps visiting his relatives, if indeed they had not broken all connections with him because of what they thought to be his apostasy from the faith of his fathers. From Tarsus they went through the famous pass in the mountains called the Cilician Gates. This pass is a great rent in the mountains running north and south for a distance of eighty miles. In all ages it has been the gate by which caravans and conquering armies passed from the central or northern part of Asia Minor to the level country by the seashore, or from the level country by the sea into Asia Minor.

Three centuries before St. Paul, Alexander the Great had come through that pass on his great invasion of the east. Now Paul the Apostle, attended by only one companion, without an army or the panoply of war, passes on foot through the same gateway, bound for the lands to the west. His passage occasioned no stir among the mountain people; yet we know now that a greater than Alexander the Great passed that day through the mountain gorge. Though he knew it not, Alexander the Great was preparing the world for the preaching of the Gospel, for his conquests spread the Greek language throughout the world, and wherever men gathered together in towns and cities, there were those who could speak and write the language of Greece. In this language the Gospels were to be written, and in this language the story of Christ was often proclaimed.

A SECOND VISIT TO LYSTRA

When the high peaks of the Taurus mountains had been left behind them, Paul and Silas took the road which led to the Lycaonian Plain and to the town of Derbe. Probably a year had passed since the first visit of Paul and Barnabas, and we can imagine the warm welcome that the Apostle and his companion would receive from those little Christian communities in the towns which they visited. From Derbe they went on to Lystra, where Paul had been worshiped as a god and then stoned and dragged out of the city for dead. On this second visit to Lystra he secured a new member of his company in the person of Timothy. As we saw in a former chapter, Timothy was the grandson of a pious Jewess, Lois, and the son of a pious mother, Eunice; but his father was a Greek. Timothy had been converted by Paul on the first missionary journey. Greatly taken with Timothy, and convinced of his earnestness and sincerity, and hearing a good report of him by the brethren at Lystra and Iconium, Paul determined to take him with him on his journey. But before doing so, he had him circumcised. Some have seen in this an inconsistent act on the part of Paul, for in the Council at Jerusalem, and in his controversy with Peter at Antioch, he had stood for the great principle of salvation by faith alone, and the inefficacy of the old law. How, then, could he, who had made such a stand against the Jewish Christians, and who had refused to circumcise his other companion, Titus, now submit Timothy to this rite of the Hebrew law? It was because Paul, although a man of principle, was also a man of common sense and expediency. If any one had insisted that Timothy had to be circumcised before he could be saved, Paul would not have done it. But he did it to help him in his work; for Timothy, as an uncircumcised son of a Jewess, would have been execrated by the Jews, forbidden entrance to the synagogues, and thus have been a hindrance instead of a help in the labors of Paul among the Jews.

The case of Timothy was quite different from the case of Titus, for Titus was a pure Greek, or Gentile, whereas Timothy was half Jew, and probably his Greek father was living. What Paul did here was in strict harmony with his desire to yield in nonessentials, if thereby he might win some to Christ. As he himself put it in his Letter to the Corinthians: "And unto the Jews I became as a Jew, that I might gain the Jews. To them that are under the law as under the law, that I might gain them that are under the law. To them that are without the law as without law, that I might gain them that are without law. To the weak became I as weak that I might gain the weak. I am made all things to all men that I might by all means save some."

Although no other cities visited by Paul on the first missionary journey, except Derbe and Lystra, are mentioned in the account of the second journey, it is probable that Paul visited Iconium

and Antioch again, where he refreshed the spirits of the converts
he had made on the first journey and delivered to them the
decree of the Council at Jerusalem. When he had passed through
the central region of Phrygia and Galatia, it was the purpose and
desire of Paul to preach the Gospel in Asia. This was the western
part of Asia Minor, and there was the great city of Ephesus. But it
was made clear to Paul that at this time he would not be permitted
to preach the word in Asia. Forbidden to preach in Asia, Paul
turned northward and traveled as far as the borders of Mysia, a
province in the extreme northwest of Asia Minor. There he planned
to go and preach in Bithynia, a populous and important province
on the Black Sea. But here again he was forbidden by the Holy
Spirit. As Luke puts it: "The Spirit suffered him not." The road to
the north had been shut against him, also the road to Ephesus.
Paul was not the sort of man who turns back. Therefore he took
the only remaining course and passed through Mysia in the direction of Troas, a town on the Aegean Sea. Troas was near the site
of ancient Troy, and all about it were the "ringing plains of windy
Troy," where Greeks had battled with Trojans. Here Alexander,
crossing from the continent of Europe, had paused to worship at
the tomb of his supposed ancestor Achilles. Here, too, Xerxes and
Caesar passed in their day of power and empire. These great
associations of world-empire and of conquest in the past, made
Troas a fit place for Paul to start on his conquest of Europe.

THE CALL TO MACEDONIA

As Paul lay in his bed that first night at Troas, perplexed, no
doubt, as to the prohibitions which the Spirit had placed upon
his labors, and wondering where God wanted him to go, there
appeared to him in a vision a "Man of Macedonia," who prayed
him saying, "Come over to Macedonia and help us." After this
record in the ninth verse of the sixteenth chapter of the Book of
Acts, the form of narrative changes from that of the third person
to the first. Henceforth for a considerable period of time the
narrative is told in the first person, "we," not "they." Since the
author of the Book of Acts is Luke, it is generally supposed that
Luke joined Paul at Troas. Some have even gone so far as to say
that the "Man of Macedonia" who besought Paul to come over

and help them was none other than Luke himself. But however interesting, this is pure conjecture and imagination. All we know is that henceforth the author of the Book of Acts is one of the traveling companions of Paul.

We thrill at the reading of this record of how Paul prepares to cross from the continent of Asia to the continent of Europe. But we must not attribute to St. Paul our own feelings, for to him it was merely passing from one part of the Greek world to another, from the Roman province of Mysia to the Roman province of Macedonia. Nevertheless, that crossing was a turning-point in the history of the human race. Paul never was disobedient to a vision from heaven, and Luke writes that "after he had seen the vision, immediately he endeavored to go into Macedonia, assuredly gathering that the Lord had called him for to preach the gospel unto them." Whether it has been an actual vision of a man of Macedonia, such as Paul had, or such as St. Patrick is said to have had when he received the invitation to cross the Irish Sea and preach the Gospel to the Irish, no great work has been done for God or man without an awakening vision of human need. Paul crossed the Aegean Sea, not to further his selfish interests or found a temporal empire, as did Alexander and Caesar and Xerxes, nor to avenge private wrong as did the Greeks when they came to make war on Troy, but to help men, to tell them the story of life and forgiveness through Christ.

We see the four men, Paul, Timothy, Silas and Luke, going on board one of the ships moored to a granite pillar in the port of Troas. The wind and tide are favorable; the ropes are cast off, the sail is hoisted, and the ship makes its way out through the harbor to the open sea where it sets its course for the island of Samothracia. Of all the expeditions which passed through those narrow seas, this was destined to be the most momentous for the welfare of our race. They soon ran by the island of Tenedos and reached Samothracia. Outside the notice given it by St. Paul, Samothracia lives in history because of the wonderful work of Greek art, the Winged Victory, which was discovered there, and which now stands at the head of the grand stairway in the palace of the Louvre. Loosing from Samothracia, after a few days run their ship reached Neapolis, which was the port of Philippi. Philippi was a settlement of old soldiers. It enjoyed the privileges of Roman citizenship and was a Roman colony, elevated to that dignity by Caesar Augustus who there conquered Brutus and Cassius. It was here at Philippi, according to Shakespeare's Julius Caesar, that the ghost of Caesar appeared to Brutus and said to him, "Thou shalt see me at Philippi." In commemoration of his own victory Octavia, or Caesar Augustus, had built at Philippi a triumphal arch. This city therefore was a fit theater for the Christian Apostle to begin his conquest of Europe.

In imagination we try to follow Paul and his three companions as they make their way from Neapolis up to Philippi and pass beneath the triumphal arch of Augustus. Everywhere they would see on the columns and pillars, public buildings and arches, the four great letters "S. P. Q. R." meaning, the Senate and People of Rome. Did they have a sense of loneliness and heaviness as they found themselves in this capital of the Roman province? Or was it with the thrill of enthusiasm and adventure that Paul found himself standing upon a new arena of his great conquest for Christ? What sublime faith and daring it required for this band of traveling missionaries to enter this city of the Roman world and have confidence that there Christ would be honored and worshiped by men. A military and political town, rather than a commercial, Philippi had little attraction for Jews, and there were not a sufficient number of them in the city to establish a synagogue. But outside of the city, on the banks of the river Strymon, they had a place of prayer where pious Jews were wont to resort to pray for the peace of Jerusalem. To this place by the river's bank, therefore, when the Sabbath day was come round, Paul and his companions went to pray. The congregation by the riverside was made up chiefly of devout women, and among them Paul and his companions sat down and spake concerning the things of Christ. In a field by the river's brink where prayer was wont to be made, and in the company of a few women, was launched the great work of preaching the Gospel to Europe. The evangelization of Europe began with a women's prayer-meeting.

Among those to whom Paul preached was one whose heart the Lord had opened, and who therefore immediately responded to the message of the Gospel. Her name was Lydia. She was not a dweller in Philippi, but had come from Thyatira, one of the cities of Asia, where she was a seller of purple garments, or the dyes used in their manufacture. This reference to Thyatira is another instance of the wonderful historical accuracy of Luke, for it is well known now that Thyatira was a place noted for the dyeing business. An ancient inscription has been found there which was set up by the Guild of Dyers, and even today Thyatira is noted for the scarlet garments which are dyed there.

The heart of man is naturally shut against the truth of the Gospel. The natural mind does not perceive the things of the Kingdom of God, and rather recoils from it. But the Holy Spirit, who was directing the work of Paul, had opened the heart of this woman to hear and to receive the word. All preaching, all evangelizing, all missionary endeavor, must be carried out in the faith and belief in the necessity of such a work on the part of the Holy Spirit, and a faith that He will do that piece of work in the hearts to whom the Gospel is preached. Lydia believed in Christ and was baptized, together with her household. As a token of her sincerity and gratitude, she invited Paul and his companions to lodge with her, saying, "If ye have judged me to be faithful to the Lord, come into my house and abide there."

The conversion of Lydia was not the work of Paul, but the work of the Holy Spirit. Nevertheless, it is worth noting that this first of European converts was a devout woman who waited upon God. Far from her native city, and engaged upon a commercial enterprise, she was yet faithful to the customs of her people, observed the Sabbath day, and went down to the riverside to pray to the God of Israel. By the riverside, outside the city of Philippi, on that memorable Sabbath morning so many centuries ago, the God who has promised to draw nigh unto them who seek Him earnestly, brought Lydia face to face with the messenger who was to tell her of Christ who would fulfill all her hopes and answer her deepest longings. Christianity has made woman immortal. Christ was born of a virgin; women were last at His cross, and first at His sepulchre; and now, of all its inhabitants, it is this devout woman who is chosen by the Holy Spirit to be the first-fruits of Europe. Henceforth Lydia has something more precious to sell and to tell than the secret of Thyatira's purple dye. Now she can tell, not of garments dyed at Thyatira, but of the Man of Nazareth, with garments dyed at Calvary.

8

AN EARTHQUAKE— WHAT SHALL I DO TO BE SAVED?

Two women are chief actors in the introduction of Christianity to Europe. One was Lydia, the purple-seller of Thyatira; the other was the slave girl who had a spirit of divination. The oratory by the riverside was the center for the preaching of the Gospel, and that was where Paul and his companions went day by day. As they went back and forth to this place of prayer, they were annoyed by a slave girl who followed them, and who had a spirit of divination, literally the spirit of a Python. The Python was the serpent worshiped at the famous Greek Oracle of Delphi, and thus the symbol of a knowledge of future events and of the unseen world. Because she was, or seemed to be, familiar with the hidden things, and could foretell the future events, the owners of this girl carried on a thriving trade with her ravings and predictions. Something in the message of Paul and his companions had attracted the poor girl, and she followed them about whenever opportunity afforded. She had sense enough to listen to the message which they preached and to get the gist of it, for as she followed them on their way to and from the place of prayer, by the riverside, she cried out with the loudness and hysteria common to the possessed, "These men are the servants of the most high God, which show unto us the way of salvation."

What the spirit of divination in the slave girl proclaimed was true. Never was there a better account given of the message of the apostles and their high office. They were, indeed, servants of the most high God, and their purpose in coming to Philippi was to show unto its inhabitants the way of salvation. It may be asked, therefore, why it was that Paul took exception to this salutation and was grieved at it, and why he commanded the spirit to come out of the girl. The chief reason, no doubt, was that just as Christ refused to accept the witness of the demons, so the apostles are not willing to have their Gospel commended, even in true terms, by one who was thought to be in league with the unseen world or with evil spirits. It is quite probable, too, that the kind of use which had been made of the maid's gift of divination, gave her a superstitious association in the minds of the people of Philippi, and that her commendation of the Gospel would be a hindrance rather than a help. Very likely the element of compassion and of pity entered into the matter also, and it is possible that Paul recognized in this possessed damsel a conflict between her disordered nature and a sincere yearning after truth and God. Therefore, he turned and said to the spirit, "I command thee, in the name of Jesus Christ to come out of her." "And he came out the same hour."

THE POWER OF THE NAME

Mighty is the name of the Lord Jesus Christ. The miracles of healing and of cleansing, which were wrought by the apostles, were always done in the name and for the sake of Jesus Christ. It is this sacred Name which ever and mightily avails with God, and when it is used by His Church in faith and in sincerity, we have the right to expect great results. Christian teachers and preachers and workers can do no better than to follow in the footsteps of the first apostles and attack the spirit of unbelief and of sin in the world in the Name of Jesus Christ, for at this Name the devils believe and tremble.

The evil spirit which was in this dazed girl described Paul and his companions as the servants of the "most high God." This name, the "most high God" was used by the legion of devils which inhabited the man of Gadara, for at the approach of Christ he cried out, "What have I to do with thee, Jesus, thou Son of the most high God?" The opposition of men in the world to

Christ often takes the form of doubt and unbelief concerning His deity and divine Sonship; but never do we find unbelief in the evil spirits, for they recognized, as did the devil himself, in the temptation of Christ, that Jesus is the Son of the most high God. It was that fact which aroused their fears and stirred their enmity and opposition. Among the evidences of the deity of our Lord, not the least striking are the testimonies from the demons.

As soon as this possessed girl was restored to her right mind and was normal in her speech and behavior, she ceased to be a commercial asset to her masters, for they could no longer employ her for revenue. This greatly enraged them against the apostles. It is a sad commentary on human nature that nothing will so arouse bitter and hostile feeling and resentment in the human breast as the loss of money. To avenge themselves on the man who had stopped their evil gains, the masters of this maid caught Paul and Silas and dragged them before the Roman magistrate, saying, "These men, being Jews, do exceedingly trouble our city, and teach customs which are not lawful for us to receive, neither to observe, being Romans." Hitherto the riots from which Paul had suffered were stirred up on the ground that his teachings were hostile to the Jews. Here we have the situation completely reversed, for the Apostles are attacked because of the fact that they are Jews.

A number of years before, the Emperor Claudius had issued a decree banishing the Jews from Rome on account of certain riots which had taken place in that city. It was always easy to stir up a tumult against the Jews, and here in Philippi, the masters of the maid out of whom Paul had cast the evil spirit, in order to get their revenge on the men who had deprived them of their source of gain, resort to the old custom, alas, also the modern custom, of Jew-baiting. Always glad to attack and beat the Jews, the multitude needed little incitement and rose up against the apostles, clamoring for their punishment. The magistrates were in sympathy with this anti-Jewish sentiment, and, without the semblance of a trial, had Paul and Silas stripped of their clothes and commanded the lictors to beat them.

In the catalogue of his woes and sufferings, Paul afterwards wrote, "Thrice was I beaten with rods." This cruel outrage at Philippi was the first of those beatings. It was a barbarous and ferocious form of punishment under which the victim not infrequently succumbed. It was the sort of scourging to which Christ Himself was subjected by Pilate, with the hope that so extreme a punishment would satisfy the Scribes and Pharisees, and thus relieve him of the necessity of sentencing Christ to crucifixion. The beating on this occasion was evidently one of unusual severity, for we read that they laid many stripes upon them.

PAUL AND SILAS IN PRISON

Faint and bleeding from their wounds, Paul and Silas were cast into prison, not the ordinary prison, but the innermost dungeon, a dark and foul den where their hands and feet and necks were made fast in the stocks. The situation of the apostles was the last word in human misery and distress. Yet at midnight, Paul and Silas prayed and sang praise unto God and the prisoners heard them singing. Paul and Silas knew the psalms, how it is written, that "God giveth them songs in the night"; and never was the promise of that psalm more strikingly fulfilled than at midnight in the dungeon of the jail at Philippi. Long afterwards, the church father Tertullian, writing to encourage the martyrs of his generation, said, "The leg feels not the stocks when the mind is in heaven. Though the body is held fast, all things lie open to the spirit." The limbs of the apostles were in the stocks and their backs were raw and bleeding from the whips of the lictors, but their minds were in heavenly places.

Out of the dungeon, they lifted a song unto heaven. What did they sing? No doubt one of the songs of David. Perhaps the Twenty-third Psalm—"Yea, though I walk through the valley of the shadow of death, I will fear no evil, for thou art with me. Thy rod and thy staff, they comfort me." Perhaps the Thirty-fourth Psalm—"I will bless the Lord at all times, his praise shall continually be in my mouth. This poor man cried, and the Lord heard him and saved him out of all his troubles. The angel of the Lord encampeth round about them that fear him and delivereth them." Or the Fortieth Psalm—"He brought me up also out of a horrible pit, out of the miry clay, and set my feet upon a rock and established my goings. And he hath put a new song in my mouth, even praise unto our God: many shall see him and fear

```
THE LORD'S VINEYARD
527 N. CHELTON ROAD
COLORADO SPRINGS, COLORADO 80909
719-597-4151

REGISTER     3
RECEIPT # 9403009942            10
DATE      03/29/94
TIME      2:07 PM

 ISBN/SPCN     PRICE  QUANTITY  AMOUNT
 9991000283      .99       1      .99
  BOOKS
 0825432693     9.99       1     9.99
  PAUL THE MAN: HIS LIFE AND WORK

                    SUB TOTAL   10.98
   SALES TAX ON 10.98 @ 6.300      .69
                  GRAND TOTAL   11.67
               PAID WITH CASH   12.00
                 CHANGE RECVD     .33

EXCHANGE, CREDIT OR REFUND WITH RECEIPT.
NO REFUND AFTER 30 DAYS.
```

527 N. CHELTON ROAD
COLORADO SPRINGS, COLORADO 80909
719-591-A1S1

REGISTER   3
RECEIPT # 9A0300394G   10
DATE   03/29/96
TIME   2:07 PM

ISBN/SPCN   PRICE QUANTITY AMOUNT
3901000683   .99   1   1.29
BOOKS
0825432543   9.99   1   9.99
PAUL THE MAN, HIS LIFE AND WORK

SUB TOTAL   10.98
GRAND TOTAL   11.87
NO REFUND AFTER 30 DAYS.

and shall trust in the Lord." Or the Forty-sixth Psalm—"God is our refuge and strength, a very help in trouble." Or the Ninety-first Psalm—"He that dwelleth in the secret place of the most high shall abide under the shadow of the Almighty. He shall give his angels charge over thee to keep thee in all thy ways. They shall bear thee up in their hands, lest thou dash thy foot against a stone. Thou shalt tread upon the lion and adder; the young lion and the dragon shalt thou trample under foot." Or the One hundred and second Psalm—"For he has looked down from the height of his sanctuary, from heaven did the Lord behold the earth, to hear the groanings of the prisoners, to loose those that are appointed to death." With songs such as these, the apostles made sweet melody unto the Lord and "all the prisoners heard them."

Suddenly, the apostles' midnight prayer-meeting was interrupted by the convulsion of a great earthquake, which shook the foundations of the prison, broke down its doors and loosed the chains from every prisoner. Philippi was in a earthquake zone, and the time and place were conspicuous for convulsions of this nature. When the jailer awakened out of his sleep and saw that the prison doors were open, he took for granted that his prisoners had escaped. A jail delivery in that ancient day was a more serious thing than it is in our day. Today it means an investigation on the part of the prison board, or the legislature, and possibly the dismissal of a jailer and his subordinates; but then it often meant death for the jailer. When Peter was delivered by the angel out of the dungeon of Herod, that cruel king commanded that all the keepers be put to death. This was the fate which the Philippian jailer expected, and therefore suicide was a common and natural resource under such conditions. Drawing his sword, he was about to fall upon it and end his life, when he heard Paul cry out with a loud voice, "Do thyself no harm, for we are all here." Paul would save men for life eternal; but if he could not do that, he would at least save men for this life startled by the prisoner's cry, and marvelling at this new kind of prisoner, who, when the doors were open, would not embrace the opportunity to flee, the astounded jailer called for a light, and sprang in, and came trembling, and falling down before Paul and Silas, cried out, "Sirs, what must I do to be saved?"

What did the jailer mean by this cry, "What must I do to be saved?" Was he thinking of the convulsion of the earthquake, or of the answer he would have to give to his Roman masters? Evidently not; the earthquake was over and his prisoners were safe. The cry was one which came out of the depths of a troubled heart, a heart which had been shaken by the earthquake of the conviction of sin. Where, then, had the Roman jailer learned the language of the Gospel? How did be know this great cardinal word of Christianity, "Saved"? He might have heard the soothsaying maid pronounce the word as she followed Paul and Silas through the streets of Philippi and declared that they had come to show the way of salvation; or he might have listened that night to some of the songs of Paul and Silas in the dungeon, when they gave God thanks for His great salvation through Jesus Christ. At all events, he knew that he was lost, and desired to know and to hear the way of salvation. Nor did he have long to wait, for they said with one breath, "Believe on the Lord Jesus Christ and thou shalt be saved, and thy house." Since the jailer knew little of Christ, this grand formula of redemption had to be followed up by words of explanation and instruction. So, we read that they spake unto him the word of the Lord, and to all that were in his house; that is, they explained to him who Christ was, what He had done for sinners on the Cross, and how faith in Christ saves the sinner.

FOCUS ON FAITH

The great doctrine with which the name of St. Paul is associated, and which is the one theme of his epistles, is justification by faith. In his epistles we see this doctrine analyzed and explained. Here in the jail at Philippi, with walls laid flat by the earthquake, we see the doctrine of justification by faith in action. The word spoken by the apostles to the trembling jailer, longing for salvation, is henceforth the motto and the charter of the Christian Church. Men are saved from sin, not by their works or by their obedience, but by faith in the Lord Jesus Christ, who by His death on Calvary made atonement for the sins of the world. Wherever true Christianity has existed, or now exists, in the world, it is but an echo of that midnight sermon, "Believe on the Lord Jesus Christ and thou shalt be saved."

The first act of this new convert was a beautiful deed of compassion and pity. We are saved by faith alone, but not by a faith which is alone. We are not saved by our works, but good works always accompany true faith. "Show me thy faith by thy works," wrote St. James. This the Philippian jailer did. As soon as he had heard and received the Gospel, he took a basin and washed the stiffened stripes and bloody wounds on the backs of Paul and Silas. Then, when he had ministered to their comfort, he received Christian baptism and all his household with him. He cleansed the wounds of the apostles inflicted by the lictors' scorpion rods, and they in turn cleansed in the waters of baptism the deeper wounds which sin had inflicted upon the jailer's soul. At midnight this jailer was a lost pagan; in the morning he was in the Kingdom of Heaven.

Meanwhile, the news of the earthquake and what had happened at the jail had reached the magistrates and their hearts were troubled. Just what led to this sudden change of front on the part of the magistrates, we are not told. Possibly the earthquake had aroused their consciences and they were disturbed at their deed of rank injustice in scourging and imprisoning these strangers without due process of trial, or any inquiry whatsoever into their history. The natural world is in league with the moral world. These men were troubled in conscience because they knew they had done wrong, and they wished, as soon as possible, to be rid of the whole matter. Therefore they sent the sergeants down to the jailer with this message, "Let those men go." When the jailer repeated the message to Paul and Silas, he got a great surprise. Far from being excited or overjoyed at this permission to leave the dungeon, Paul said, "They have beaten us, openly, uncondemned, being Romans, and have cast us into prison: and now do they thrust us out privily? Nay verily; but let them come themselves and fetch us out."

Never in all his stormy career did the noble pride and self-respect of Paul find a more magnificent expression. Paul was a free-born Roman citizen, and therefore, by this right of Roman citizenship, was exempted from degrading punishment such as that of scourging. And doubly heinous was it for a magistrate to punish and imprison a Roman citizen without inquiry or trial. The words "Civis Romanus sum," "I am a Roman citizen," in that day often stayed the hand of the oppressor and the robber. It may be asked why Paul had not stood on his right of Roman

citizenship when he was scourged by the lictors, as he did when
the captain of the guard at Jerusalem threatened to scourge him.
Perhaps in the turmoil and excitement, he was not able to make
himself heard, and it is unlikely that the magistrates themselves
were present, but gave their haughty and cruel order to the
lictors, who would pay no attention to any claim of Roman citizenship on the part of Paul or Silas.

But now, when the sergeants take the word back to them that
Paul is a Roman citizen, the magistrates are frightened. If their
consciences before had troubled them because of their act of injustice in beating and imprisoning the apostles without due process of
trial, now their fears are aroused because they know that their act
was not only morally, but legally, wrong. Hence the magistrates
themselves came down to the prison in answer to the proud de-
mand of Paul, who had said that he would not go out privily, under
cover of the early dawn, like a guilty criminal, but would leave the
jail only in the custody of the magistrates themselves. To these
proud terms the conscience-stricken and frightened magistrates
agreed and coming down to the jail respectfully requested Paul and
Silas to depart out of the city. With all his yearning desire to save
others and his wonderful sympathy for people, Paul never once
demeaned himself or lowered the flag of his manhood. He would be
"all things to all men" if thereby he might save some; but he would
permit no man to wipe his shoes on him, and always, on every
occasion, he maintained the high dignity of the human spirit.

Having been conducted out of the jail, Paul was in no hurry to
leave the city. He went first to the house of Lydia, which was the
headquarters for the little Christian colony which had sprung up.
There he greeted the brethren and comforted them, and then
departed for Amphipolis, thirty-three miles south of Philippi. In
the recital of these stirring events at Philippi, we have no mention of Luke or Timothy, who had come to the city with Paul and
Silas. Less conspicuous than the other two, Luke and Timothy
seem to have escaped the wrath of the mob, and were neither
beaten nor imprisoned. Brief as was Paul's stay at Philippi, it
marked the beginning of the most tender and cherished of all his
church relationships. This was the Church he loved above all
others, and long years afterwards, he could write to them, "I have
you in my heart."

9

THESSALONICA—TURNING THE WORLD UPSIDE DOWN

Starting from the Forum at Rome, a number of great highways traversed Italy, leaped over the ocean, and invaded the territories of the Roman provinces, coming to an end only at the frontiers of the Empire itself. Divided by milestones, and running from one city to another, piercing mountains and bridging chasms, these great roads united one part of the Empire with another. They were paved with large blocks of stone, and in many places have survived the traffic of almost two millenniums. One of these great roads, the Via Egnatia, led from Philippi across Macedonia to the Adriatic Sea, where communication was had with Italy by ship. It was by this famous road that Paul and Silas set out from Philippi for Thessalonica, one hundred miles to the west.

Their wounds from the scourging still raw, and their joints still swollen from the stocks, it must have been with no little suffering that the two followers of Christ made their way over the white dusty highway toward Thessalonica. Their first stop was at Amphipolis, thirty-three miles from Philippi, and the next at Apollonia. There being no Jewish population of any size at either city, and therefore no foothold for the apostles, they pressed on to the more important and more populous metropolis, Thessalonica, where, Luke tells us, was a synagogue of the Jews. This city was named after Philip of Macedon's daughter, and was a place of considerable importance at the head of the Thermaic Gulf, and no little commerce passed through its port.

Thessalonica was the place of Cicero's exile in 58 B.C. Gazing one day at the summit of distant Olympus, Cicero exclaimed with a mingling of satire and sadness, "I see nothing but snow and ice!" It was at Thessalonica, too, that the Emperor Theodosius, in the year 390, in a tempest of rage because of a riot, had his soldiers slaughter seven thousand of the inhabitants of the city, regardless of rank, sex or guilt. For this deed of monstrous cruelty Ambrose, the Bishop of Milan, refused the Emperor the communion and repulsed him from the altar of the Church. Eight months afterwards Ambrose gave him absolution after he had promised in the future not to execute a death penalty until thirty days after the procuring of the sentence.

An Important Center

As Paul and Silas neared the city to pass through the archway at the entrance, they saw a numerous and great company issuing from or entering the city. Haughty Roman legions, the sun flashing on their eagle helmets and round shields; or the chariot of a general of the army; brown men from Egypt, black men from Africa, Barbarians from the Danube and Jews from Jerusalem, philosophers from Athens, senators from Rome. No one paid the slightest attention to Paul and his companion. Yet that evening there passed through the triumphal gates at the entrance to the city and into Thessalonica the man whose visit and whose brief letters to the Church which he founded there will give Thessalonica its chief claim to fame.

Through the narrow crowded streets, resounding with the cries of traders and drovers, Paul and Silas threaded their way until they reached the Jewish quarter of the city, where they entered the humble home of Jason. This Jason was a distant relative of Paul, and is mentioned by him in the letter which he afterwards wrote to the Romans. Although lodged in the house of a relative, Paul was careful not to be a charge to any one at Thessalonica, and, as he tells us in his letters to the Church in this city, "did not eat bread for nothing at any man's hands," but "in labor and travail worked night and day that he might not be a burden unto any of them." In the house of Jason, or at some other convenient place, Paul worked at his trade of a tent-maker, using the periods of rest for his discussions of the Gospel, and especially the rest period of the Sabbath days. As his custom had been in the other cities which he had visited, Paul went into the synagogue on the Sabbath day, and using the Old Testament as a basis for his preaching, declared that, according to the prophecies, Christ was to suffer and die, and rise again from the dead. He then brought his message to its climax by declaring that this Jesus whom he preached was the Christ, the Messiah.

In following this manner of preaching Paul modeled his preaching after that of Jesus Himself, who during the period between His resurrection and His ascension, "Beginning at Moses and all the prophets, expounded unto them in all the Scriptures the things concerning himself." As a result of the preaching there were many who believed, and followed Paul and Silas, especially of the higher minded Greeks, and among them, a considerable company of the "chief women." Again, as at Philippi in the case of Lydia, and afterwards at Athens in the case of Damaris, we see women taking an important place in the spread of the Gospel in Europe.

A SERIES IN THE SYNAGOGUE

For three successive Sabbaths Paul preached in the synagogue, and the company of those who believed grew from day to day and from week to week. But the Jews who believed not and were moved with envy at the reception given to the Gospel by the Greeks and the Gentiles of the city, stirred up men of the baser sort, the dregs and rabble which are to be found in any great commercial city, and sowing false suspicions in their minds, played upon their passions until the mob, beside itself with wild unreasoning fury, surged down on the Jewish quarter and battered the house of Jason, where they expected to lay hold of Paul and Silas.

Fortunately, Paul and Silas were not at that time in the house of Jason. Either they were absent on some Gospel errand, or they had heard on the afternoon air the cries of the infuriated mob as it rushed toward the house of Jason. Failed in their efforts to seize Paul and Silas, the mob laid hold of Jason and certain disciples found at his house and dragged them before the rulers of the city, crying out, "These that have turned the world upside down are come hither also, whom Jason hath received; and these all do contrary to the decrees of Caesar, saying that there is another king, one Jesus." To say that the apostles were preaching not only an illegal religion, but were declaring "another king," was a most serious charge. From what Paul wrote afterwards in his letters to the Thessalonians, we know that his preaching on this occasion had a great deal to say about the kingdom of Christ and the glory and the power of His Second Coming, "when he should be revealed from heaven with his mighty angels, in flaming fire, taking vengeance on them that know not God, and who obey not the Gospel of the Lord Jesus Christ." It would not have been strange if, misapprehending this reference to Jesus, some of the populace of Thessalonica actually thought that Paul was declaring a rival king and a rival Empire. The Jews who instigated the riot probably knew better; but they were quite willing to play upon the ignorance and misunderstanding of the rabble.

Both of the charges shouted by the mob were true of Paul and Silas, but not in the sense in which the mob meant them. They were men who were turning, and would yet turn, the world upside down, for wherever they had gone riots and disorder had broken out because of the natural enmity of man to the mind of God. Above all the kings and empires of this world they were declaring another king, even Jesus, whose kingdom was not of this world, but an everlasting kingdom which should have dominion from sea to sea and from the river unto the ends of the earth. Christ is the king of the nations and of human society. He does not come into the world merely to choose followers and disciples out of it; He comes into the world as its sole and rightful sovereign. He is the ruler and governor among the nations. The authority of Christ was rejected then, and He is still rejected and disowned by this world.

> Our Lord is now rejected,
> And by the world disowned,
> By the many still neglected,
> And by the few enthroned.

Both as to His person and as to His precepts, Christ is rejected. "We have no king but Caesar," was the cry of the Scribes and Pharisees at Jerusalem, and of the mob of Philippi and Thessalonica; and that cry is still echoed by the unbelief of the world today. The second Psalm, written so many ages ago, still describes our world today: "The kings of the earth set themselves, and the rulers take course together against the Lord, and against his anointed, saying, Let us break their bands asunder and cast their cords from us."

The magistrates rebuked Jason and his companions for having given hospitality to such agitators and troublers of the peace, and compelled them under bond to guarantee the quick departure of Paul and Silas from the city. Thus terminated the visit of Paul to Thessalonica. During his stay of several weeks in that city, Paul, although laboring early and late to supply his own necessities, received timely aid from the thoughtful and generous disciples at Philippi, who, he says, "sent once and again" unto his need. One of the notable converts at Thessalonica was Aristarchus, who was a companion of Paul on his later journeys, and was with him at Ephesus, Jerusalem and Rome. Since Jason had given bonds for their immediate departure, on that same night, when the passions of the mob had cooled somewhat, friends in Thessalonica conducted Paul and Silas out of the city and started them on the road to Berea, fifty miles to the south, near the seacoast.

The traveler today to Salonica, the modern successor to ancient Thessalonica, finds himself in the midst of a tawdry, tumble-down, unkempt Turkish town, although it is now under the government of Greece. When the intolerable heat of the day has passed, the visitor who strolls along the waterfront will see before him the incomparable blue bay of Salonica, and in the distance the great shoulders of the brown mountains, and just where the sun is sinking, the highest peak of them all, Mount Olympus, the fabled abode of Homeric deities. Slowly, slowly, the sun goes down, until the mountains are lost in the gloom of the night.

The sunset on Olympus seems to tell of the sunset of paganism and idolatry. Mount Olympus has been eclipsed by another mount, Mount Calvary; the mount where the gods laughed and wantoned, and drank their nectar, has been replaced by the mount where God suffered and died for the sins of the world. Standing there on the shores of the wonderful bay, and watching the sun go down behind Mount Olympus, the traveler who is familiar with New Testament history thinks of the celebrated visitor who once came to Thessalonica to tell the story of Mount Calvary. On the night air he can hear again the wild cries of the angry mob as they rush Jason and his companions to the judgment seat of the magistrate, "These that have turned the world upside down have come hither also, saying that there is another king, one Jesus." The herald of that king had to flee the city by night in order to save his life. Yet the Gospel of that king, wherever it has reached and transformed human life, has turned the world upside down.

ON TO BEREA

In Berea Paul had a kinder reception than he had met with in Thessalonica, for Luke writes that the "Bereans were more noble than those of Thessalonica, in that they received the word with all readiness of mind, and searched the Scriptures daily, whether these things were so." They gave the Gospel at least the respect of comparing it with what was written in the prophecies of the Old Testament. The result was that many believed, and here again, as at Thessalonica, a great company of honorable Greek women. But the enemies of Paul were still on his trail, and as soon as the Jews at Thessalonica learned where he was, and what he was doing at Berea, they came there also and roused the people against him. In order to save him from the violence of the mob, the disciples, without waiting for the storm to break, conducted Paul down to the seacoast to the port, where he took ship for Athens. Silas and Timothy, who in the meantime had rejoined Paul after he was separated from them at Philippi, were left behind at Berea. That it was safe for them to remain in the town showed that the persecuting fury of the Jews and their Gentile agents was directed chiefly against Paul.

The goal of Paul was Athens, distant from the port of Berea about three days' sail. The faithful companions who had conducted him from Berea and now received his affectionate farewell, and a message from him to Timothy and Silas to join him at Athens as soon as possible, stood on the shore and watched the small coasting vessel on which Paul bad taken passage, sail out of the harbor into the Gulf of Therma, until the ship was but a mere speck on the horizon, and then was lost altogether to their sight. If they were sorry to see Paul leave them, we know that Paul too was sad and troubled at heart, for although he had been separated from Silas but a few hours, and from Timothy but a little season, he yearned already for their companionship, and left an urgent message for them to come to him with all speed at Athens. With its square sails spread, slowly rising and falling with the gentle pulse of the Aegean, and the wind from the mountains blowing softly, the ship with every league draws nearer to the sacred land of Greece.

10

ATHENS—THE ALTAR TO THE UNKNOWN GOD

On the first part of the voyage from Berea to Athens, Paul's ship skirted the mountainous and rugged coast of Macedonia. For the greater part of a day the mighty summit of Mount Olympus, and then Pelion and Ossa, were visible from the deck of the ship. On the second day the vessel entered the narrow strip of sea which separates the mainland of Greece from the long and singular island of Eubeca. Now with every tack the ship was grazing the shores of classical Greece. Toward the close of the second day, or on the morning of the third, the ship must have sailed close by a great plain with mountains in the distance, and if Paul had been gazing in that direction, as he probably was, he could have seen in the midst of the plain the great mound which was heaped over the dead who fell in the battle of Marathon, 490 B.C., where the Greeks under Miltiades routed the vast host of the Persians.

Some writers have taken the view that Paul was totally ignorant of the great history which had been enacted on those shores which he was passing, and that Marathon and Thermopylae and Salamis would mean as little to him as Gettysburg or Bunker Hill to a South Sea Islander. But to this view we do not subscribe. Since he spoke the Greek language fluently, and was able to quote some of its literature, and was brought up in a city where there was much Greek life and culture, Paul, an intelligent man, must have been familiar with the great outlines of Greek history. It is true that his own sacred land was elsewhere, and that "the wisdom of Javan" was to Paul as nothing compared with the revelation which had been granted to Israel.

GLORIOUS GREECE

Before the ship was able to steer a course to the north and enter the harbor of Athens, the Piraeus, it had to round the rugged promontory of Sunium. If the day was clear, or still better, if the night was clear and the moon shining, Paul and those with him on the vessel could have seen high up on the furthermost rock of the promontory a beautiful white temple with massive Ionic columns. This was the temple of Neptune, one of the glories of the Greek world, and today, even in its crumbling and half-ruined state, this temple, more than any other relic of Greek art and worship, tells the traveler of the "glory that was Greece."

Passing these memorable and sacred places, and sailing amid islands and waters of incomparable beauty, Paul's vessel carried him to Athens. The traveler who today follows in the wake of Paul's ship, beholds the same blue sky, the same gently heaving Aegean, the same historic shores, the white columns of the same temple of Neptune, and everywhere, the isles of the sea, girt with the foam of breaking waves. Looking upon those isles, and thinking of the past of Greece, there comes to the traveler's mind those words of a great friend of modern Greece, Lord Byron:

> The Isles of Greece, the Isles of Greece
> Where burning Sappho loved and sung,
> Where grew the arts of war and peace,
> Where Delos rose and Phoebus sprung.
> Eternal summer gilds them yet,
> But all except their sun is set.

Long before he reached the Piraeus, indeed, even off the promontory at Sunium, Paul could see the sun flashing on the bronze helmet of the great statue of Minerva, which stood alongside the Parthenon on the Acropolis at Athens. From the Piraeus to Athens is about an hour's walk. As Paul made his way toward the famous shrine of art, science, literature and politics, he passed many a tem-

ple, many an altar, and many a statue and image. The world has
seen three famous cities, Jerusalem, Athens, Rome. Athens gave the
world art; Rome gave the world law; Jerusalem gave the world God.
Therefore, Jerusalem was, and is, incomparably the greatest of the
three. Paul had already trod the streets of Jerusalem. In a few years
he will pass down the Appian Way and enter the Roman Forum.
Now he enters Athens, the city of the mind.

When Paul entered Athens, the sun of Greece had set. It was
four hundred years since the Parthenon had looked down upon
the Athens of Socrates and Plato and Phidias. Athens now was not
even the political capital of the Roman Province of Greece, for
that distinction had been given to Corinth, a much more populous
and commercially important city. But so far as art and philosophy
were concerned, Athens was still the capital of the world. The
wonderful creations of her great artists still stood in all their glory,
unshaken by time and undefiled by the hand of man.

When Paul came to Athens his spirit was stirred within him,
but not in the way in which the spirit of a modern traveler stirs
within him when he approaches that famous city, that is, with the
memories of Demosthenes and Socrates and Plato. What stirred
and troubled the spirit of Paul was to see the great city given
over to idolatry. Paul had been born and brought up in a pagan
city, Tarsus, and in his travels through Asia Minor and in Macedonia he was constantly in sight of heathen altars and idols. It
was not the novelty of the thing which now stirred him, but the
universality, the ubiquity of it. It was an ancient saying that in
Athens it was easier to find a god than it was to find a man. Paul
was a Hebrew of the Hebrews, and to him even the most beautiful of these creations of art were but repulsive exhibitions of the
spirit of idolatry and gross violations of the Second Commandment. Aroused by the idolatry in which the city was immersed,
Paul spoke against it, and declared the true God and His only
Son Jesus Christ, preaching every Sabbath day in the synagogues,
and daily in the marketplace.

SIDELINED IN ATHENS?

It was not Paul's original plan to spend any length of time at
Athens. His special call had been to preach the Gospel in Mace-

donia, and in obedience to that call he had met with marked success at Philippi, at Thessalonica, and at Berea. Persecution had driven him first out of Philippi to Thessalonica, and then out of Thessalonica to Berea, and then from Berea to Athens. But he was still hopeful that he could soon return to Thessalonica. To him Athens was only a waiting place until he could get back to Macedonia. In the great city of the Athenians Paul was lonely and ill at ease. When he said farewell to the Berean disciples, as his ship sailed for Athens, he charged them to tell Timothy and Silas to come to him speedily at the latter city. Now he is waiting for them to come. There is no place so lonely or depressing as a great foreign city. The very multitudinous life which ebbs and flows about a man seems to mock his spirit, for he realizes that he could lie down and die there and not a single sigh be breathed at his passing and not a single tear be shed. What with the absence of his friends, and the multitudes of idols, Paul was troubled and depressed in spirit.

But he was not a man to lie idle, especially in a great city where men were worshiping images. On Sabbath days he addressed himself to the Jews. On week days he entered the marketplace where everything was bought and sold, from a horse to a book of poems, and finding plenty of well-educated idlers and loiterers, he declared to them the mystery of the Gospel. He had no difficulty in getting an audience and a hearing, for he was able to speak fluently the Greek tongue, though probably with a provincial accent. The intensity of his utterance and the solid matter of it, and the novelty of it, guaranteed him a company of listeners; for, as Luke says, with perhaps a Macedonian scorn of the Athenians, "All the Athenians and strangers which were there spent their time in nothing else but either to tell or to hear some new thing." Long before Luke wrote this, Demosthenes had said, "We Athenians stay at home doing nothing, always delaying and making decrees, and asking in the market if there be anything new." This love for gossip is still a national trait, and to this day the traveler in Athens will see a great company of men and women sitting at their tables, in Constitution Square, morning, noon, or midnight, either telling or hearing some new thing.

THE TEACHINGS OF THE STOICS

Among those who listened to Paul preaching, were certain philosophers of the Epicureans and of the Stoics. The Stoic school of philosophy was founded in the fourth century B.C. by Zeno, in Cyprus, who taught on a Stoa, or porch, in the market-place; hence the name, Stoic. The Stoics were pantheists and recognized a great force working everywhere which they called God, but which they did not recognize as a person, but as a fire and mist which permeates all things, calling men into existence and destroying them again. With them the highest good was virtue.

They taught resignation, restraint and self-control in all things. Among the Stoics were Epictetus, Seneca, and Marcus Aurelius. The Epicureans were founded by Epicurus in the fourth century. They recognized no Creator, but accounted for all things by changes in the eternal atoms. They preached pleasure, but, in the early representatives of Epicureanism, the pleasures, not of the body, but of the mind and the spirit. With much that was noble and worthy in them, these two schools had degenerated with the process of time, Stoicism tending to fatalism and the worship of suicide, Epicureiism to the glorification of lust.

From the account that we have of his preaching elsewhere, we know that Paul had a great deal to say about Jesus and the resurrection. So prominent a place did this doctrine of Jesus and the resurrection have in his daily preaching in the marketplace, that some of those philosophers who heard him took him to be a babbler and wind bag, while others thought that he was setting forth some new god, probably taking Jesus and the resurrection as a male and female deity. Athens was ready to recognize almost any god from any part of the world. But before a new god could be worshiped and proclaimed, the court of Areopagus had to pass on its claims. From what took place on Mars Hill before this august tribunal, the court before which Socrates was tried, and on the same indictment, that he was setting forth strange gods, we cannot be sure whether Paul was asked merely to state his views before the judges of that court, or whether he was actually on trial before them as a proclaimer of new gods. It is not altogether improbable that the latter was the case.

THE SERMON ON MARS HILL

Mars Hill is a considerable elevation on the west side of the Acropolis. As Paul took his stand on that day in the midst of the celebrated court, he could see in front of him the noble marble gateway to the Acropolis, the Propylaea, and crowning the rock, five hundred feet above the level of the sea, the glorious temple to the Virgin goddess, Athena; and by the side of the temple the great bronze image of Athena, holding in her hand the mighty spear moulded out of the trophies taken from the Persians at the battle of Marathon. Such then was the stage upon which Paul stepped forth to play his part and deliver his memorable speech, a speech which men will know and read and ponder long after the studied eloquence of Demosthenes and Plato and Socrates shall have been forgotten. It is altogether probable that what we have recorded of that speech in the Acts is only a brief outline, or summary, of what Paul said. But even in this abbreviated form, it is a magnificent utterance.

"Ye men of Athens, I perceive that in all things ye are too superstitious, for as I passed by and beheld your devotions, I found an altar with this inscription: To The Unknown God. Whom therefore ye ignorantly worship, him declare I unto you. God that made the world and all things therein, seeing that he is Lord of heaven and earth, dwelleth not in temples made with hands, neither is worshiped with man's hands as though he needed anything, seeing he giveth to all life and breath and all things, and hath made of one blood all nations of men for to dwell on all the face of the earth, and hath determined the times before appointed, and the bounds of their habitation; that they should seek the Lord, if haply they might feel after him, and find him, though he be not far from every one of us: for in him we live, and move, and have our being; as certain also of your own poets have said, For we are also his offspring. Forasmuch then as we are the offspring of God, we ought not to think that the Godhead is like unto gold, or silver, or stone graven by art and man's device. And the times of this ignorance God winked at; but now commandeth all men everywhere to repent: Because he hath appointed a day, in the which he will judge the world in righteousness, by that man whom he hath ordained; whereof he hath given assurance unto all men, in that he hath raised him from the dead."

The introduction to Paul's speech paid a delicate tribute to the religious interest of the Athenians, and yet at the same time had in it the shadow of a rebuke. Our English word "superstitious" brings out only the rebuke, whereas the more frequent translation, "very religious" brings out only the compliment. What Paul said was a mingling of praise and blame. He will talk to this picked audience of Athenian philosophers with all courtesy and consideration; yet he will be careful not to say a word which might be construed as a justification of idolatry. Paul was charged, either generally, or in a judicial sense, with declaring a new god. He answered this charge by saying that he was proclaiming the true God, to whom he found an altar in their midst, with this inscription: To the Unknown God. In heathen cities this was not an uncommon thing. Lest any god should be overlooked, and thus his good will be lost, the idolaters erected altars not only to the gods whom they knew by name, but to unknown gods. When Paul took those words on the Greek altar "To the Unknown God," for his text, he did not mean to say that the Greeks had built an altar to Jehovah, the true God, nor did he mean to say that God cannot be known, and that the Greeks with their altars had come as near to the true worship as the Jews or the Christians who worshiped the living and the true God. On the contrary, he took the legend as a confession on the part of the Athenians of the inadequacy of their worship, and that with all their altars and temples they had failed to find the true God. But this God, who was unknown to the Athenians, was made known to men through Jesus Christ. This is the God whom Paul now declared. It was this Greek word, "To the Unknown," that Huxley took and turned into the English form "Agnostic," that is, a man who says of religion and of God, "I do not know."

GOD AS CREATOR

Let us now see what Paul thought worth declaring about the Unknown God. In the first place, he declared that this God was the Creator. Where the Bible commences, there Paul began: "In the beginning, God." "God that made the world and all things therein, and hath made of one blood all nations of men." There were special reasons why some of his philosophers needed to know that primary truth about God, the Creator of all, for by their theories they dispensed with God as the Creator and beginner. There, then, Paul starts: God made the heavens and the earth and created man in His image. The world is not eternal and it is not accidental. It came into existence through the will and the power of God, who is not a part of nature, but above it and beyond it and before it. "Before the mountains were brought forth, or ever thou hadst formed the earth and the world, even from everlasting to everlasting thou art God."

This truth of God as Creator is no outworn fragment of Christian truth. It is a truth which is just as timely and necessary for this generation as for the Greeks in the days of St. Paul. The first article of the Christian creed is, "I believe in God the Father, maker of heaven and earth." Having commenced with the doctrine of God as Creator, St. Paul then stated two great inferences of this doctrine: first, that such a God does not dwell in temples and cannot be served with altars and men's hands, "as though he needed anything." The magnificent boldness of this utterance is appreciated only when we remember where it was made, not in London, or Paris, or New York, but in the very heart of ancient Athens, with the temple of the Parthenon and the bronze image of the goddess Athena towering over him.

Paul's motto as a preacher, whether in Jerusalem, Athens or Rome, was always "Woe is me if I preach not the Gospel!" Courteously and earnestly, but plainly, clearly and firmly he told the Athenians that so far as an approach to God was concerned, there was nothing at all to all their gods and altars; even the lovely temple of Athena was not the home of God, for "He dwelleth not in temples made with hands." The second great inference of his doctrine of God as Creator was the unity of the race and the solidarity of the human family. "God hath made of one blood all nations of men." Again, to get the force of this, one must remember who spoke it, to whom it was spoken, and where and when it was spoken. The Jews divided the world into Jews and Gentiles, and the Greeks into Greeks and Barbarians. But here was an Hebrew of the Hebrews, of the straitest sect of the Pharisees, within the very shadow of the Acropolis, surrounded by the glories and monuments of a boasted Greek superiority and difference, saying to the philosophers that God hath made of one blood all nations of men, and that the differences of nations and races and men are as nothing compared with their identities. This fact of the physical oneness of humanity Paul uses as a parable of a higher spiritual fact, the moral unity of the race. Since God was the Creator and Father of all, therefore all men were one, and since Christ died for all, all had need of His atonement.

GOD AS RULER

The second great truth about God, brought out in Paul's speech, was the doctrine of God as the ruler and upholder of the world. He says that not only did God create the race, but that He presides over its history and its destiny. He did not make the world and leave it, but He has determined beforehand "the times before appointed and the bounds of their habitation, that they should seek after God." Greece was not an accident, any more than Jerusalem was an accident, or Rome or the United States of America. The most eloquent preacher of all is history, with her great and awful voice. The great movements of history are not without the permission of God, nor do they fail to register His will. The drama of time is God's drama, and the great men, the great nations, the great movements and crises of history are but the "brief embodiment or the transient realization of His will." Musing on the plain of Sedan, where Germany crushed France in 1870, Victor Hugo wrote: "In the terrible shadow, O Thou Invisible One, I saw Thee."

GOD AS JUDGE

The third and last truth about God declared by Paul in his great sermon was that God is our Judge. He is the Creator of men, the Father and preserver of men, the sovereign ruler of men, and He is our Judge. "The history of the world is the judgment of the world." This is a profound truth. But Paul goes beyond this fact of general and natural religion, and declares a final judgment of the world by Christ. God, he said, has had long patience with the race, passing over their times and seasons of ignorance and disobedience, but at the close of the human drama there is a stop, and that period is the day of judgment. "God hath appointed a day, in which he will judge the world by righteousness, by that Man whom he hath ordained." To this solemn fact, that there is a judgment, and that Christ is the Judge, and that all men shall appear in that judgment, Paul declared that the resurrection of Christ was the irrefragable witness: "whereof he has given assurance to all men, in that he hath raised him from the dead."

When he spoke of the resurrection, and the judgment which follows, and how all men must repent, Paul had reached the climax of his sermon. But beyond this he was not permitted to go. The philosophers had heard him patiently when he declared the great truths with which they had some general familiarity and sympathy, creation, providence, and the unity of the race; but when he came to talk of the resurrection and of judgment they mocked at him. Who was this crazy philosopher who told them that in the day of judgment they must give an account of the deeds done in the body, and that their only hope for escape from sentence was faith in Jesus, who had been crucified and raised again from the dead the third day?

With expressions of laughter, mockery and disgust, the assembly broke up, and Paul sadly made his way down the steep descent to the humble home where he was lodged as a guest. But if most of them mocked, and the rest of them said they would perhaps hear him about the matter on another day, there were some to whom Paul did not preach in vain. Among them was one of the judges of the court, Dionysius, and "a woman named Damaris."

11

CORINTH

Corinth is forty miles from Athens, and in going to that city from Athens, Paul had the choice of two routes. He could go by land and cross the isthmus, or he could go down to the Piraeus, the port of Athens, and there take a ship across the Saronic Gulf to Cenchrea, the port of Corinth. If he took the land route, he would pass on the way to the Isthmus of Corinth, Eleusis, the seat of the ancient mystery religion of Greece. If Paul was familiar with the history of this shrine, when he passed it he must have reflected upon that far greater mystery, which it was now his privilege to declare unto the world, the mystery of the Gospel of reconciliation, hid from times eternal, but now declared unto men through Jesus Christ. The probability is that Paul took the sea route, going from the Piroeus to Cenchrea. Cenchrea, like most ports, was a collection of shops and inns for sailors. From Cenchrea it was a journey of nine miles to Corinth.

Long before he reached the city of Corinth, Paul could see towering in the distance the Acrocorinthus, the lofty citadel of Corinth. This mountain rose above the plain and the sea to the height of almost half a mile. At its northern base lay Corinth. This was not the Corinth of Greek antiquity, but a new city which had been built on the ruins of the old by Julius Caesar. The new city, like the old, was a place of great commercial importance. This was due to its singular location. The Peloponnesus, the southern portion of Greece, almost an island, is joined to the main continent by a narrow strip of land called the Isthmus, the Bridge of the Sea, and this same name, isthmus, or neck, has been given to every similar body of land throughout the world, such as the Isthmus of Panama, the Isthmus of Darien, and the Isthmus of Suez. This isthmus was the gateway to the Peloponnesus, and likewise the gateway to northern Greece. Armies of invaders coming from the north or coming from the south had to pass that way. On one side of the isthmus, to the west, was the Gulf of Corinth, and to the east, on the other side, was the Saronic Gulf. On each Gulf, and not far from Corinth, was a port, Cenchrea, the port connecting Corinth with the Aegean Sea, and Lechaeum, connecting it with the Adriatic. Corinth was situated at the southern end of the isthmus, and thus it was that trade and commerce, whether coming by land or by sea, had to pass through its gates. It was this which made Corinth one of the great commercial cities of the world.

In 146 B.C. Corinth, which was then a dependency of Rome, was destroyed by the Proconsul Mumius, because of the outbreak of a rebellion. In the conflagration which destroyed the city it was said that the accidental fusing of certain metals led to the discovery of the famed Corinthian brass. For more than a century Corinth lay desolate; but in 44 B.C. the city was repeopled and rebuilt by Julius Caesar; and when Paul arrived there in 52 A.D., it was again a thriving metropolis and the seat of the government of the Roman province of Achaia. The city was noted for its luxury and its immorality. More than a thousand prostitutes practiced their shameful trade at the temple of Venus under the veil of religion and worship. The very name of Corinth was a synonym for licentiousness, and "to Corinthianize" meant to lead a dissolute life. Even the Christian community which was founded at Corinth by Paul showed traces of the licentiousness which made the city notorious, for in a letter which he afterwards addressed to the Corinthian Christians, Paul deals with shocking instances of gross immorality, such, he declared, as could not be found even among the pagans.

Paul's experience at Athens was not such as would have exalted his spirit. Outwardly, his mission there had been a failure, and it is not strange therefore that we find him approaching the city of Corinth with a degree of misgiving and depression of spirit. In the first letter which he afterward wrote to the Corinthians, he reminds them how he came first to Corinth "in weakness and in fear, and in much trembling." When Paul reached a city or town on his missionary journeys, his first concern was to secure a suitable lodging, and then employment by which he could earn his daily bread. Living at Corinth in the Jewish colony were two Jews, Aquila and his wife, Priscilla, who had been driven out of Rome by the decree of Claudius. A Roman historian tells us riots had taken place among the Jews at Rome, and that the leader of them was "Chrestus," and that because of these riots the Jews were expelled from the city. It is altogether probable that by "Chrestus" the historian meant Christus, or Christ, and that because of the dispute among the Jews over Christ, a mistaken opinion had arisen that Christ was the leader of a faction of the Jews.

AQUILLA AND PRISCILLA

Aquila and Priscilla had come to Rome from Pontus, the rich province on the Black Sea. They were evidently on their way home again when they stopped at Corinth, and there, in the midst of that populous city, found employment, for they were, like Paul, tent-makers. In their house, therefore, Paul found lodging and also employment. In Corinth, as at Thessalonica, Paul made every effort at independence, lest any should charge him with a mercenary motive in preaching the Gospel. But even his utmost exertions at Corinth in his calling as a tent-maker, were not sufficient for his self-support, and in the letter which he wrote from Corinth to the Thessalonians, Paul acknowledged the gift which they sent him through Silas and Timothy, and especially the gift which had come from his beloved friends at Philippi: "When I was first with you and was in want, I was not a burden on any man, for the brethren when they came from Macedonia supplied the measure of my want, and in everything I stopped myself from being burdensome unto you. And so will keep myself."

In daily contact with Paul, Aquila and Priscilla heard the message of Jesus and Him crucified and embraced the new faith. Of them we shall hear frequently in Paul's subsequent journeys, for we find them at Ephesus, and again at Rome. In the letter which he wrote long afterward to the Church at Rome, Paul sent greetings to his friends Aquila and Priscilla, and says of them that they laid down their necks for his own life, and that unto them is due, not only his own thanks, but that of all the churches of the Gentiles.

SILAS AND TIMOTHY

Meanwhile, Silas and Timothy, who had been left at Berea and at Thessalonica, came to join Paul at Corinth. At Corinth, as at Athens, Paul was still hoping that the door would be opened for him to return to Thessalonica; but in this he was disappointed. However, Timothy and Silas brought him good tidings from Thessalonica that the disciples there were standing fast in the faith and that through them the Gospel was sounding out through all Macedonia. But there were some things which they told Paul about the Church at Thessalonica which gave him concern. The Thessalonian Christians were perplexed and troubled about the fate of their friends who had died in Christ, and wondered if they were not to share the great blessing which He would shortly bestow at His second coming. There were some, too, who were upset in their minds by the teachings of the apostles about the second coming of Christ, so much so that they were refusing to work, neglecting their daily business in expectation of the appearance of the Lord. To comfort those who were mourning concerning the dead, and to warn and admonish those who were leading excited and disorderly lives, Paul wrote the two letters to the Thessalonians. These letters are the earliest of his epsitles, and the earliest documents of the New Testament. They are the first rivulets of the mighty stream of New Testament inspiration.

In the first letter, in words ever precious to the Church, Paul comforts the mourning disciples and assures them that their beloved dead will share in the blessings of Christ's advent. He says:

"But I would not have you to be ignorant, brethren, concerning them which are asleep, that ye sorrow not, even as others which have no hope. For if we believe that Jesus died and rose again, even so them also which sleep in Jesus will God bring with him. For this we say unto you by the word of the Lord, that we which are alive and remain unto the coming of the Lord shall not prevent them which are asleep. For the Lord himself shall descend from heaven with a shout, with the voice of an archangel, and with the trump of God: and the dead in Christ shall rise first:

Then we which are alive and remain shall be caught up together with them in the clouds, to meet the Lord in the air: and so shall we ever be with the Lord. Wherefore comfort one another with these words."

In the second letter Paul speaks of certain things which must come to pass before Christ will appear, such as the falling away, or apostasy from faith, and the revelation of the man of sin and antichrist. The disciples had been upset and excited by false teachings as to the coming of Christ, and we infer from what Paul writes that forged letters, as if from him, had partly accounted for their misunderstanding. He says:

"With regard to the arrival of the Lord Jesus Christ and our muster before him, I beg you, brothers, not to let your minds get easily unsettled or excited by any spirit of prophecy or any declaration or any letter purporting to come from me, to the effect that the Day of the Lord is already here. Let nobody delude you into this belief, whatever he may say. It will not come until the Rebellion takes place first of all, with the revealing of the Lawless One, the doomed One, an adversary who vaunts himself above and against every stalled god or object of worship, actually seating himself in the temple of God with the proclamation that he himself is God."

All that Paul meant by these references was, of course, much more clear to the Thessalonians than it is to us as we read the letters nineteen centuries afterwards, for Paul speaks of that concerning which he had already given instructions to the Thessalonians, saying: "Do you not remember, I used to tell you this when I was with you?" The best that we can do now is to conjecture what the falling away is to be, and who the man of sin and the lawless one are. To the Thessalonians there was no doubt as to what Paul meant when he used these names.

Every Sabbath, as his custom had been in other towns, Paul went to the synagogue and reasoned with the Jews, and also on the streets, as he had opportunity, with the Gentiles. The coming of Timothy and Silas from Thessalonica and Beraea greatly strengthened him and encouraged him for his work. Luke writes that "Paul was pressed in the spirit, and testified to the Jews that Jesus was Christ." The word "pressed," is the same as that employed by Jesus when He said, "I have a baptism wherewith to be baptized, and how am I pressed until it be accomplished." His preaching to the Jews evidently met with a opposition and hostility unusual even with them; for when they opposed and abused him and blasphemed the name of Jesus, Paul shook out his garments as a protest against them, saying, "Your blood be on your own heads, I am not responsible; after this I will go to the Gentiles." Here again, as in the towns where he had visited in Galatia, Paul gave the Jews the first opportunity, and then, with words of warning on his lips, turned from them to the Gentiles.

CONVERTS AT CORINTH

Next to the synagogue of the Jews lived a man named Justus, one who was probably a proselyte, that is, a Gentile who had become a Jew. Into his house, Paul entered and from day to day preached the Gospel to all who would hear. The first of his converts was Epeanetus, whom he called the first fruits of Achaia. Other notable converts were Crispus, the chief ruler of the synagogue, and Gaius. The reason why Paul did not baptize the converts at Corinth was because of the danger of his being charged with baptizing them in his own name and building up a personal following or faction. The converts at Corinth were, for the most part, men of humble rank, and those who had been sunk in iniquity and evil customs. "Behold," wrote Paul to them afterwards, "your calling, brethren, how that not many wise after the flesh, not many mighty, not many noble, are called." There as always, the Gospel of Christ was able to save unto the uttermost. After naming the vices common to the Corinthians, such as idolatry, adultery, sodomy, drunkenness and thieving, Paul says significantly, "Some of you were once like that; but you washed yourselves clean, you were consecrated, you were justified in the name of our Lord Jesus Christ, and in the Spirit of our God."

The advent of a new governor in a Roman province was an event of the greatest interest and importance to the people whom he was to rule. The new governor, or Proconsul, for the Roman province of Achaia was Gallio; he was a brother of the famous Seneca, the tutor of Nero, and like his brother, was born in Cordova, in far-off Spain. Seneca gives to his brother a fine character, and pays him a beautiful tribute when he says of him, "Whom every one loved too little, even he who loved him most."

The Jews being exceedingly enraged against Paul thought they would try out the new governor by bringing forward charges against Paul. The conversion of the chief ruler of their synagogue, Crispus, and the daily preaching of the Gospel in a house next to the synagogue, undoubtedly greatly excited and alarmed the Jews, and it is certain that Paul's life was in constant danger at their hands. It was in this crisis that Paul received one of those visions which God granted to him in his hours of need. In a vision the Lord appeared unto him by night and said to him, "Be not afraid, but speak and hold not thy peace, for I am with thee, and no man shall spit on thee to hurt thee, for I have much people in this city." This assurance gave Paul confidence and he continued his work in Corinth for a year and six months.

When Gallio made his appearance, the Jews stirred up a riot, and dragging Paul before the judgment seat of the governor, charged him with inciting men to worship God contrary to the law. This was a serious charge, and Paul was about to open his mouth in his defense as he had done at Athens. But Gallio judged from what the Jews had said that the whole thing had to do with some dispute as to Jewish custom, doctrine and belief. For the Jews and their doctrine he had only contempt, and before Paul could make any statement by way of defense, Gallio quashed the indictment, saying, "If it had been a misdemeanor or wicked crime, there would be some reason in me listening to you, O Jews; but as these are merely questions of words and persons and your own law, you can attend to them for yourselves. I decline to judge upon such matters as that." So saying, he ordered them to leave his court. The disappointed Jews were slow to leave, and the Greek hangers-on who had gathered to see the sight, hearing the governor's contemptuous dismissal of the case, took advantage of the opportunity to vent their hatred of the Jews, and laying hold of Sosthenes, the chief ruler of the synagogue, beat him in front of the judgment seat. "But," says Luke, "Gallio cared nothing for these things." That comment on the indifference of Gallio has often been taken to mean his utter indifference to higher things and to the claims of religion.

But there is little ground for such an indictment. Gallio thought that he was dealing merely with technicalities of Jewish law, and with an incident of Jewish bigotry and vindictiveness. He cared nothing for these things. Little could the Proconsul have guessed the significance of the prisoner who stood before him or the message which he had to preach. Little could Gallio have foreseen that nineteen centuries after he drove the Jews away from his tribunal, he would be remembered only because Paul had been brought into his court. Paul remained for some time after his acquittal at Corinth, but as the season wore on, he had a longing to go to Jerusalem in time for the Passover. Therefore, taking with him his friends and his hosts, Aquila and Priscilla, he went down to Cenchrea and there took ship for Ephesus.

While at Corinth, Paul had taken the vow of the Nazarites. It was customary for a pious Jew in the time of sickness or of danger to pray for deliverance and to take upon himself a vow which was to be performed when deliverance was granted. This vow involved abstinence from wine, and letting the hair grow long. St. Paul claimed liberty for himself with regard to all the Jewish customs; but the fact that he took upon himself such a vow shows that he was a child of his race and still adhered to many of the Jewish customs. It is possible, too, that the knowledge that he had taken such a vow would commend him to some of the Jews whose prejudices he had to encounter.

The particular occasion of Paul's vow we are not told. Perhaps it was a safe deliverance from peril at Corinth. That he was in great peril there we know from the vision which he had and the assurance given him that none should set upon him to do him harm. Or the occasion of the vow may have been serious illness. When Paul, on a subsequent visit to Corinth, sent his famous letter to the Church at Rome, through the Deaconess Phoebe of Cenchrea, he commended her to the Christians at Rome as "A succourer of many, and of myself also." It is quite possible that Phoebe nursed Paul during a period of sickness at Corinth, for Cenchrea was close at hand. The Nazarite vow was usually performed by cutting the hair at Jerusalem and burning it at the altar for a peace offering. Yet a certain liberty was allowed to Jews who had to travel a great distance.

FROM CORINTH TO EPHESUS

With Aquila and Priscilla for his companions, Paul took passage
on a sailing vessel which was in the trade between Corinth and
Ephesus. Cicero says that on a similar voyage from Corinth to
Ephesus the vessel took fifteen days, and on a westward trip, thir-
teen days. This was an unusually long passage, and with good weather
the ship on which Paul was traveling would have made the journey
to Ephesus in much shorter time. Being bound for the feast at
Jerusalem, Paul did not plan to tarry at Ephesus, and the fact that he
stopped there for only a few days and left there his companions,
Aquila and Priscilla, may have been due to the opportunity which
Ephesus afforded Aquila and Priscilla for the sale of their tent cloth.

At Ephesus, a vast and populous city, where many Jews were in
residence, Paul entered into the synagogue and reasoned with
them. His reception was very favorable, and they were anxious to
have him remain with them for a longer period. This Paul would
not consent to do, telling them that he was on his way to keep the
feast at Jerusalem; but he promised them that he would return and
tell them more about Christ and the Gospel. In this promise Paul
made fitting and beautiful recognition of the purpose and providence of God in his life, for he said, "I will return again unto you,
if it is the will of God." He who in his great doctrinal statements
gives us the sublime teaching as to the purpose and the predestination of God in human life, here, in such a saying as this to the
Jews at Ephesus, shows us the practical effect of this doctrine in
his own life. His life was not an accident, but a great plan of God.
All his own plans and purpose were contingent upon the will of
God.

As soon as the ship on which he had sailed was ready to leave
port again, Paul boarded it and set sail for Caesarea. On this
voyage he passed Coos and Rhodes with its famous Colossus.
Then the ship ran along the southern coast of Asia Minor, probably stopping at Patara and Myra, and thence made the long run
through the open sea to the southwest of Cyprus, until it reached
Caesarea. From Casarea Paul went up to Jerusalem. Luke tells us
nothing of this visit, merely saying that he "saluted" the Church
and went down to Antioch. This was Paul's fourth visit to Jerusalem. The first was when he spent fifteen days with Peter after his

return from Arabia; the second when he took a collection from Antioch up to Jerusalem for the disciples there who were suffering from the famine; the third when he went up with Titus and Barnabas to attend the council at Jerusalem which had been called to decide the standing of the Gentile Christians; and now this fourth visit at the close of the second missionary journey.

One of Paul's reasons for going to Jerusalem was the observance of the Passover. That he was willing to take the Nazarite vow on himself, and that he was anxious to keep the feast at Jerusalem shows how the old piety and faith still had a place in the religious life of St. Paul. Although called to be the Apostle to the Gentiles, and a victim of cruel assault and wicked slander on the part of the Jews, Paul's heart was still with his people, and he could truthfully say, "Brethren, my heart's desire and prayer to God for Israel is, that they might be saved. . . . I say the truth in Christ, I lie not, my conscience also bearing me witness in the Holy Ghost, that I have great heaviness and continual sorrow in my heart, for I could wish that myself were accursed from Christ for my brethren, my kinsmen according to the flesh."

After the celebration of the Feast of the Passover, now, through the institution of the Lord's Supper, invested with a new and sacred meaning for the Jewish disciple, Paul went down to Antioch, going either by land to Caesarea, and thence by ship up the coast to Antioch, or by land the entire distance. Antioch was now the center for the missionary activities of the Church, and there Paul began to plan and dream still greater conquests for Christ.

12

EPHESUS—
FIGHTING WITH BEASTS

When Paul stopped at Ephesus on his way from Corinth to Jerusalem, he promised his friends there, that, if the Lord willed, he would return and pay them a longer visit. When he set out from Antioch at the beginning of the third great missionary journey, Ephesus was his chief objective. On his way to Ephesus he passed through Galatia and Phrygia, visiting churches which he had founded on the first and second journeys, confirming their faith, and taking from them a collection for the relief of the poor at Jerusalem. Luke does not tell us how Paul went to Galatia, from Antioch.

Two routes were open to him, that by sea to Perga, and thence over the mountains to Galatia, or by land to Tarsus, and thence through the Cilician Gates into Galatia. The latter was probably the route followed by Paul. At Lystra, Derbe, Iconium and Antioch of Pisidia, Paul had joyful reunions with the disciples in the churches of those cities. Some he found in sorrow over friends, who had died since he last was there, and them he comforted with the assurance that those who slept in Jesus, God would raise up at the coming of Christ. Others, he found giving heed to false doctrines which led them to trust for salvation in something else than Christ and Him crucified. Them he reminded of their former zeal for truth, their early affection for him, and told them that there was only one Gospel, the Gospel of Christ crucified, and that if even an angel from heaven should preach any other Gospel, or any other Christ, "Let him be accursed." We cannot be sure whether Paul's great letter to the Galatians was written before or after this visit, but we can be certain that in this visit to the churches of the cities of Galatia Paul said substantially what he wrote in his epistle. If even to read his words as they stand at the conclusion of his letter to the Galatians, thrills us after the lapse of so many centuries, we can imagine how powerful such an utterance must have been when pronounced orally to the Christians of a city such as Lystra, where Paul had been stoned and dragged out of the city for dead. For example, such words as these, "Far be it for me to glory, save in the cross of our Lord Jesus Christ, through which the world has been crucified unto me and I unto the world.... From henceforth let no man trouble me, for I bear branded on my body, the marks of Jesus."

A MEMORABLE MINISTRY

When he had finished his work in Galatia and Phrygia, Paul came to Ephesus. This great city had been the goal of his desire, when he had set forth on the second missionary journey. But when he attempted to pass from Galatia into Asia, the province of which Ephesus was the capital, the Spirit of God hindered him. Now, however, that inhibition had been lifted, and Paul was permitted to commence what was perhaps the most memorable three-years ministry of his whole life. Great and rich as it was in ancient days, Ephesus is famous today because there St. John probably wrote the Book of Revelation and spent his declining years; there St. Paul labored for three years, and there he penned the matchless lyric on Divine Love, the thirteenth chapter of First Corinthians.

Together with Rome, Alexandria and Antioch, Ephesus was one of the four great cities of the world of Paul's time. It was favorably situated near the mouth of the River Cayster, not far from the Aegean Sea. Its harbor, long since silted up and closed by the deposits of the River Cayster, was then ample and commodious, and ships from all parts of the Mediterranean world lay at anchor in the roads or were tied fast to the docks. Well located to catch the trade of the sea, Ephesus was not less favorably located with regard to the overland commerce which the caravans brought to her gates, for Ephesus was the western terminus of great caravan routes leading to the north and eastward to Mesopotamia and to India. Every caravan that wound its way over the desert, every ship that rose and fell with the swell of the Aegean or the Mediterranean, contributed to the wealth and prosperity and splendor of Ephesus. There are passages in the Book of Revelation which seem to reflect St. John's familiarity with the great city on the River Cayster, for instance, where he describes the commercial wealth of Babylon: "The merchandise of gold and silver and precious stones, of pearls and fine linen and purple and silk and scarlet and all thyine wood, and all manner of vessels of ivory and all manner of vessels of most precious wood and of brass and of iron and of marble and cinnamon and odors and ointments and frankincense and wine and oil and fine flour and wheat, sheep and horses and chariots and slaves, and souls of men." John's dramatic climax to the long catalogue of things bought and sold in Babylon was true of Ephesus, as of every other great city of the world. There, souls of men and women were bought and sold. To set free some of those souls, and to translate them from the kingdom of Satan to the Kingdom of Light, Paul had come to Ephesus.

The public buildings of Ephesus were in keeping with the wealth and the population of the city. They were constructed of white marble quarried from the near-by Mount Prion. Tradition had it that a shepherd named Pixodoros was one day watching his flocks on the mountain side, when two of his rams began to fight. One charged the other, missed him, and rammed the rock hard by, breaking off with his horns a piece of pure white marble. The shepherd carried the fragment back to the city, and the people were delighted to discover that so beautiful a stone was just at hand for the building of the temple of Diana.

Diana's temple was rated as one of the Seven Wonders of the World and was the most notable and the largest of all the temples of the pagan world. A temple had been built at Ephesus during the reign of Croesus, richest of all kings. This temple was destroyed by a fire kindled by the fanatic Herostratos in 356 B.C., the day of Alexander the Great's birth. By firing the temple Herostratos hoped to attain an immortality of fame. The fact that his name is mentioned in this book, almost twenty-three hundred years since he put his torch to the temple, is proof of how he succeeded. In order to secure a firm foundation and guard against the danger from earthquakes, epidemic in that part of the world, hides and wool and charcoal were rammed by piles far down into the marshy soil. Upon these strong foundations rose the majestic temple. The platform upon which the temple stood measured 425 feet in length and 239 feet in width. The length was about the same as that of St. Paul's Cathedral, the width just twice that of St. Paul's. But when we give the dimensions of an ancient temple, we must not think of such a temple as all under one roof, like our modern churches and cathedrals. The temple consisted rather of a series of colonnades and courts and approaches, all centering about the inner chapel or shrine which housed the altar of sacrifice and the idol of worship and veneration. At Ephesus this inner temple, the temple proper, measured 342 feet in length and 164 feet in width, four times as large as the temple of Athena, the Parthenon at Athens. The ancient coins of Ephesus show the temple to have been a building not unlike the Parthenon. In the front and rear were two rows of eight columns each, and on either side of the sanctuary, two rows of twenty columns. Each column was a monolith of marble, 55 feet in height. Eight of these magnificent jasper columns can be seen today in the Mosque of St. Sophia, at Constantinople, where they were transported by the Emperor Justinian after the destruction of Ephesus by the Goths in 260 A.D. The temple was all glorious within with the paintings and sculptures of Praxiteles, Apelles and Phidias. The doors were of carved cypress wood surmounted by vast transoms, and the stairway which led to the roof had been made of a single gigantic vine from Cyprus. The roof was covered with large white marble tiles, and to the sailors on the decks of ships approaching the harbor, the temple gleamed in the distance with the brilliancy and beauty of a star.

A DESCRIPTION OF DIANA

All this glory of architecture was for the sake of a hideous wooden block, the image of Diana. Although the name used was the same, we must not identify this Diana with the "Chaste Huntress" of Greek mythology, with bow and arrow, and the hound at her feet. The coins from ancient Ephesus show the idol to have been not unlike a mummy, one end the head of a woman with her arms extended and supported by props. In order to convey the idea of fertility, the upper section of the idol was covered with female breasts and the lower portion of the body with the representations of various animals. Such then, was the image of Diana which the Ephesians worshiped and which they believed had fallen down from heaven.

Other notable buildings in Ephesus were the great theater, the largest in the world at that time, accommodating fifty-five thousand people, and the stadium, or circus, where the games and gladiatorial shows were staged. During his long stay in Ephesus, Paul no doubt was quite familiar with temple, theater and stadium. From what he heard or saw of the games in the theater and stadium, Paul borrowed many of those figures of speech which appear in his letters, such as "Pressing toward the mark for the prize of the high calling of God in Christ Jesus"; "fighting not as one who beateth the air"; "keeping the body under"; "striving for an incorruptible crown." In his very last message to the world, the letter to Timothy, Paul tells how he expects shortly to receive the crown of righteousness, which, unlike that given to the victor in the stadium or arena, does not fade away. It is interesting to note also, how in the letter which he wrote afterward to the Christians at Ephesus, Paul makes use of the temple thought of man's body; "and are built upon the foundation of the apostles and prophets, Jesus Christ himself being the chief corner stone, in whom all the building fitly framed together, groweth unto a holy temple in the Lord." The First Letter to the Corinthians was written from Ephesus, and in that letter also Paul makes use of this temple thought of man, his body and his nature—"Know ye not that your bodies are the temple of the Holy Ghost?"

Aquila and Priscilla, the two friends with whom Paul had lodged during his stay at Corinth, and whom he had left at Ephesus on his way up to Jerusalem, had by this time established themselves in their trade at Ephesus, and it must have been in their home that Paul again took up his lodgings. Some time before Paul reached Ephesus, there had come to that city a certain Jew named Apollos, a native of Alexandria in Egypt, an eloquent man and mighty in the Scriptures. He had come in contact either with John the Baptist, or the disciples of John, and had received the baptism of John. He knew the preaching of John, that the Messiah was to come and that He was near at hand, but was ignorant of the fact that He had come. Aquila and Priscilla beard him speaking with boldness and eloquence in the synagogue, and seeing in him one who could be of great service to the Kingdom of Christ, took him apart and "expounded unto him the way of God more perfectly." When he had received information as to the message of the Gospel, he was sent with letters of introduction to Corinth, where he quickly made a name for himself, inspiring and helping all those who had been converted from Judaism and paganism to Christ, and mightily convinced the Jews, showing by the Scriptures that Jesus was Christ. At Corinth Apollos unwittingly became the center of a faction, for in that city there arose different groups, some claiming to follow Paul, some Peter, and some Apollos. We hear nothing more of him, save a reference in Paul's second letter to the Corinthians, which would seem to indicate that Apollos had returned again to Ephesus, and a mention of him in Paul's letter to Titus, where he tells Titus to set forward Zenas the lawyer and Apollos on their journey.

TWELVE NEW DISCIPLES

In Ephesus Paul found a group of twelve persons, who like Apollos, knew only the baptism of John. When he asked them, "Have ye received the Holy Ghost?" they replied, "We have not so much as heard whether there be any Holy Ghost." The only difference between those twelve uninstructed disciples at Ephesus and multitudes within the Christian Church today is that whereas those disciples had not heard of the Holy Ghost, the disciples of today have heard of Him, and that is about all. Paul asked these men unto whose name they were baptized, and they answered, "Unto John's baptism." Paul explained to them the difference between the baptism of John and the baptism of Jesus, how the baptism of John was the baptism of repentance, whereas the baptism of Jesus was the baptism of repentance, and faith in that One to whom John had testified.

Those twelve men neglected the Holy Spirit through ignorance. Multitudes in the Church today neglect the Him through indifference. We are not asked to explain the high mystery of the

Trinity, or the relationship which the Holy Spirit bears to the other Persons of the God-head. The main thing for us to ask ourselves is, Have we received the Holy Spirit? Are we resisting His influence? Are we obeying His voice in our worship and in our prayers? Do we recognize Him, and His presence and His administration of the affairs of the Kingdom of Redemption?

For three months, Paul taught and disputed with the Jews in the synagogue. But when some of them showed an inveterate hostility to the Gospel and blasphemed Christ and the Gospel before the multitude, Paul followed the course he had taken at Corinth, and withdrawing from the synagogue, established his headquarters in the school of Tyrannus. Tyrannus was probably a teacher of rhetoric, a convert to the Gospel, and Paul availed himself of his lecture hall during the hours when the classes of Tyrannus were not meeting. With this place for his preaching center, Paul preached the Gospel to Ephesus and to all that part of Asia. It is quite probable that all the Seven Churches of Asia were established at this time. Paul had many companions with him, Titus, Timothy, Gaius, Aristarchus, Sosthenes, Tychicus and Trophimus. Either going in person during his three years' stay, or through these representatives, and by the pilgrims who came up to Ephesus to worship Diana and went away worshiping the true God, even Jesus Christ, Paul was able to reach all that part of Asia.

During his stay in Ephesus, Paul supported himself by his own labors as he had done at Corinth, and not only himself but some of his companions who were with him, for he said afterwards in his beautiful farewell address to the elders of the Church at Ephesus, "Ye yourselves know that these hands have ministered unto my necessities and to them that were with me." It was a period of intense and fervent personal and public ministry, for he could testify that he had kept back nothing that was profitable, and how he taught them publicly and from house to house, declaring unto them all the counsel of God, and how by the space of three years he had ceased not to warn every one, "night and day, with tears."

DEALING WITH DEMONS

At Ephesus, Paul was mighty not only in words, but in works, and through him great miracles were wrought. So great became his fame in this respect that whenever he laid aside the apron which he used at his tentmaker's task, or a handkerchief, it was snatched up by those standing around and carried to their sick friends. In this connection, there occurred a dramatic incident which had the greatest effect in the furtherance of the Gospel in Ephesus. Ephesus was one of the chief homes of the black art, and all sorts of fakirs, impostors, charlatans, sorcerers and fortune tellers swarmed in the city. Among them were certain degenerate Jews, the seven sons of one Sceva, a chief priest of the Jews. These men went into the house of a man possessed with an evil spirit and tried to cast out the demon in the name of Jesus whom Paul preached. The evil spirit answered at once, "Jesus I know and Paul I know, but who are ye?" When he had thus said, the man possessed of the demon leaped on them, and though they outnumbered him seven to one, overcame them so that they fled out of the house, naked, wounded, and glad to escape with their lives.

This became known throughout the city and great reverence was paid to the name of Christ. "Fear fell upon them all, and the name of the Lord Jesus was magnified." Many of those who had been resorting to witches, sorcerers and fortune tellers, or themselves had been plying the black art, brought their books and charms and talismans and burned them in the center of the city. It was estimated that the value of the books and articles so consumed amounted to ten thousand dollars. An interesting parallel is afforded in the history of Florence, when, under the spell of the eloquence of Savonarola, the well-to-do people brought their articles of vanity and human folly and burned them in the public square.

Paul was planning to go on into Macedonia, thence to Corinth, back to Jerusalem again, and from Jerusalem to Rome. He had sent Timothy and Erastus ahead of him into Macedonia, and was himself preparing to follow, when there occurred the event which almost cost him his life. One of the chief sources of income for the silversmiths of Ephesus was the fabrication and sale of small silver models of the temple of Diana. Through the preaching of St. Paul, with its lifting up of the true God as alone worthy of worship, there had been a serious falling off in the market sales of the silversmiths. What a tribute to the power of the Gospel! Here was an obscure, wandering Hebrew preacher who had to toil night and day at making tent cloth for his living, with only two or three equally obscure companions, preaching and teaching under the shadow of the greatest heathen temple in the world. And yet, such was the power and truth of his message that the silversmiths of Ephesus began to fear for their trade.

THE SPEECH OF DEMETRIUS

One of the leaders of the silversmiths, Demetrius by name, called together all the workmen of his union or guild and made them the following inflammatory speech:

"My men, you know this trade is the source of our wealth. You also see and hear that not only at Ephesus but almost all over Asia this fellow Paul has drawn off a considerable number of people by his persuasions. He declares that hand-made gods are not gods at all. Now the danger is not only that we will have our trade discredited but that the temple of the great goddess Artemis will fall into contempt and that she will be degraded from her majestic glory, she whom all Asia and the wide world worship."

This clever speech by Demetrius appealed, first of all, to the greed and covetousness of the workmen on the plea that their means of a livelihood was endangered, and secondly, to their superstition and habits of worship, sowing in their minds the idea that their goddess Diana was being despised, and that her magnificence would shortly be destroyed. Stirred up by this oration, the silversmiths ran out on the street from their meeting place full of wrath against Paul and the Christians, crying out, "Great is Diana of the Ephesians." The loungers and loiterers and lewd men of the baser sort quickly took fire and joined in the uproar. The mob charged through the streets in the direction of the house of Aquila and Priscilla where they knew that Paul lodged.

Paul was either absent, or hearing their approach when the mob came roaring to the doors of the house, escaped through the loyalty and courage of Aquila and Priscilla. Paul said afterwards that for his sake, they "laid down their necks." This must have been the occasion of their courage and sacrificial loyalty, fronting the wrath of the mob while Paul made his escape. Unable to lay hold of Paul, the leaders of the mob seized upon his two companions, Gaius and Aristarchus, and dragged them into the great theater where the public assemblies were held, with the purpose of going through some form of a mock trial and putting them to death. But the multitude was so great, and the confusion so widespread, and the shouting so clamorous that they were not able to carry out their purpose. The greater part of those who jammed the theater did not know what it was all about, some shouting one thing, and some another.

In the meantime, Paul, having learned that his two friends and companions in travel, Gaius and Aristarchus, had been dragged to the theater, was resolved to go there and suffer whatever fate befell his faithful friends. But the disciples who had him in safe-keeping would not suffer him to go forth, and their protest was seconded by that of certain influential friends of Paul, the Asiarchs, the seven wealthy men who had charge of the games and the public spectacles. The Jews who had rushed with the mob into the theater, hearing that the anger of the mob was against those who had denounced idols, and knowing that in the popular mind, the Jews were associated with an abhorrence of idols, began to fear that they were the objects of the hostile demonstration and put forward one named Alexander to make a defense on their behalf. Alexander took the stand and stretched forth his hand intending to make a speech. But when the people saw by his face and heard by his accent that he was a Jew, they set up a great roar, crying out again, and for the space of two hours, "Great is Diana of the Ephesians."

In his last letter to Timothy, Paul warns him against one Alexander the coppersmith, who, he says, did him much harm. It is quite probable that this Alexander is to be identified with the Alexander who was put forward by the Jews to make a speech in their behalf in the theater at Ephesus. As for Demetrius, the silversmith who stirred up the trouble, some have identified him with the Demetrius whom John speaks of in his Third Letter as follows: "Demetrius hath good report of all men, and of the truth itself. Yea, and we also bear record and ye know that our record is true." John probably wrote this letter from Ephesus, and it is not at all unlikely that the Demetrius who stirred up the riot against Paul had become a convert to the Gospel.

The riot was still at its height, the theater echoing with the roars and cries of the mob, when the town clerk, or recorder, arrived on the scene, and quickly sensing the situation, took the rostrum and delivered the following speech:

"Men of Ephesus, who on earth does not know that the city of Ephesus is Warden of the temple of the great Artemis and of the statue that fell from heaven? All this is beyond question. So you should keep calm and do nothing reckless.

"Instead of that, you have brought these men here who are guilty neither of sacrilege nor of blasphemy against our goddess. If Demetrius and his fellow tradesmen have a grievance against anybody, let both parties state their charges; assizes are held and there are always the proconsuls. Any wider claim must be settled in the legal assembly of the citizens. Indeed there is a danger of our being charged with riot over today's meeting; there is not a single reason we can give for this disorderly gathering."

It was a very able and clever speech, and quickly quelled the riot. He dismissed as preposterous the idea that any one, especially a strolling Hebrew preacher like Paul, could endanger the temple or the worship of the great Diana. If they had real charges against Paul and his companions, they could file these charges in the courts and have them heard in due process of trial. To gather together in such an uproar, and under these illegal conditions, was full of danger to them and the whole city, for it might reach the ears of the Proconsul, and high Roman officers, as all the world knew, were not over-gentle or over-scrupulous when it came to dealing with a riot of the people. With this appeal both to the vanity and to the common sense of the multitude, the recorder put a stop to the disorder and the assembly broke up.

ENCOUNTER AT EPHESUS

In the letter which he wrote to the Corinthians shortly after his departure from Corinth, Paul referred to his trials and dangers at Ephesus, saying, "We would not, brethren, have you ignorant of our trouble which came to us in Asia. We were pressed out of measure, above strength, insomuch that we despaired even of life. But we had the sentence of death in ourselves that we should not trust in ourselves, but in God which raiseth the dead, who delivered us from so great a death, and doth deliver. In whom we trust that he will yet deliver us." It is possible that the peril to which he refers here was the riot of the silversmiths in the theater at Ephesus. But there are also reasons for thinking that the reference is to some other danger and peril through which he had passed.

In his First Letter to the Corinthians, in the great chapter on the resurrection of the body, Paul says, "If, after the manner of men, I have fought with beasts at Ephesus, what advantageth it me?" The argument of the Apostle is that if there is no resurrection of the body and no life after death, all his sufferings and hardships in behalf of Christ have been in vain. He might far better have said with himself, "Let us eat, drink and be merry, for tomorrow we die." There were many other perils and hardships through which Paul passed in his career as an ambassador for Christ, such as the stoning at Lystra, and the beating with rods at Philippi, but he mentions the encounter with beasts at Ephesus as the most trying of all his experiences. If this was a real encounter with beasts in the circus at Ephesus, the allusion has great force. But if it was merely a superstitious case, the argument falls flat. In the reference that he makes to his trials at Corinth, Paul clearly intimates both a desperate danger and trial and a miraculous deliverance. It may well have been, therefore, that Paul was actually put into the arena at Ephesus to fight with beasts, and that in some wonderful, but unrecorded manner, he was delivered from so terrible a death.

13

UP TO JERUSALEM, BOUND OF THE SPIRIT

While Paul was having his wonderful ministry at Ephesus, he had not forgotten the churches of Macedonia and Greece. Corinth was within easy communication of Ephesus, and Christian disciples coming from Corinth to Ephesus brought Paul news of the Church at Corinth. Among those who came with tidings from the Church there were members, or slaves, of the household of Chloe, one of Paul's converts at Corinth. The news which they brought him was disturbing and distressing. It told of a very unhappy condition which had arisen in the Church there. The disciples had divided themselves into groups and factions— some calling themselves followers of Paul, others followers of Peter and others, followers of Apollos.

There were also unseemly disorders, even rioting and drunkenness, at their love-feasts and at the celebration of the Lord's Supper. But worst of all was the immorality of some of the members of the Church. It was reported to Paul that a man was even living with his stepmother, and while his father was alive, a form of incest which Paul says was unheard of even among the pagans. It was not actual incest, for the man and the woman had no blood relationship; but it was a heinous offense against decency and the honor of the family. In order to deal with this extraordinary case, and also to give instruction on the general subject of marriage and social purity, Paul wrote his First Letter to the Corinthians. In this letter he directed the Church to assemble itself and discipline the offender who had disgraced the Gospel: "In the name of our Lord Jesus Christ, when ye are gathered together, and my spirit, with the power of our Lord Jesus Christ, to deliver such an one unto Satan, for the destruction of the flesh, that the spirit may be saved in the day of the Lord Jesus." In this message to the Church at Corinth, Paul refers to an earlier epistle which he had directed to them, and which dealt with similar questions. This epistle has been lost. Although occasioned by a gross case of immorality, this First Letter of Paul to the Corinthians is forever memorable as containing the great chapter on the resurrection of the body and the wonderful hymn to Christian Love.

STOPPING IN TROAS

After dispatching this letter, Paul followed it by sending a messenger in the person of Titus. He was evidently greatly distressed about further news which had come to him concerning the conditions in the Church at Corinth and the attitude of the Christians there toward his instructions to discipline the offender. The frequent references to Titus and his visit in his Second Letter to the Corinthians reveal the keenest anxiety and distress on the part of Paul. When he left Ephesus he went to Troas, where he was to meet Titus on his return with tidings from the Church at Corinth.

It was at Troas that Paul had seen the man from Macedonia in his dreams, and answering the call, had crossed to Macedonia and commenced the evangelization of Europe. Resting now at Troas, Paul must have recalled the vision of that memorable night and how much he had seen and suffered and done for Christ since then. The riverside prayer-meeting, the maid with the spirit of divination, the jail and the stocks and the earthquake at Philippi, the mobs at Thessalonica and Berea, the sea voyage to Athens, the speech on Mars Hill, the long stay in Corinth, the hearing before Gallio, the friendship of Aquila and Priscilla and Phoebe, the journey up to Jerusalem by way of Ephesus, then down to Antioch, and the long journey through Galatia and Phrygia to Ephesus, the three years of labor there, the great dangers through which he had passed, the sentence of death, the fighting with beasts—all this had taken place since Paul last slept at Troas. Here he tells us

a great and effectual door was opened for him. It was the one time
in his career that Paul did not enter such a door. The reason was
his great distress of mind about the Church at Corinth.

After waiting for some time at Troas for Titus to come, Paul
says that he found no rest in his spirit and sailed from Troas into
Macedonia, going, no doubt, to Philippi and Thessalonica. There,
too, he was in great perturbation of mind, for he tells us that his
flesh had no rest. "We were troubled on every side, without were
fightings, within were fears." But at length his anxiety came to an
end with the coming of Titus. "Nevertheless," he says, "the God
that comforteth those that are cast down comforted us by the
coming of Titus." Titus brought him good news about the obedience of the Church at Corinth, how they had disciplined the
offender and carried out the commands of Paul. Paul's chief anxiety now is concerning the disciplined offender, lest they should be
too severe with him, and writing the Second Letter, he charges
them to forgive and to restore the excommunicated person, "lest,"
he says, "Satan should get an advantage from it." It is a beautiful
instance of Paul's zeal for the purity of the Church on one hand,
and his deep sympathy and compassion for the transgressor.

Never in his whole career does Paul reveal such joy, such a sense
of deliverance, such exuberance of spirit as in this Second Letter,
where he refers to the news which Titus had brought from Corinth.
"Now thanks be unto God," he says, "who always causes us to
triumph in Christ." Nothing less splendid than a Roman triumph
will do to illustrate the freedom and joy of his spirit. No longer
depressed in spirit, harassed and anxious, Paul likens himself to a
Roman conqueror riding at the head of his troops in his chariot
along the Via Sacra through the capital and to the temple of Jupiter
amid the cheers of the populace, the fragrance of garlands and the
incense from the altars, with captives and prisoners in his train. Paul
frequently referred to himself as the slave of Christ, the prisoner of
Christ. Now he likens himself to a Roman Conqueror. Through
Christ he had come off conqueror and more than conqueror.

CALLING FOR A COLLECTION

One of the chief objects of Paul's visit to Macedonia and Greece
was the gathering of a collection for the poor at Jerusalem. The

reasons for his emphasis upon this collection were threefold. First, the wish of the pillars of the Church, as stated in the decree of the Council of Jerusalem, that he should remember the poor; second, to bring about a good understanding between the Jewish and the Gentile factions of the Church at Jerusalem; and third, Paul's desire to atone for his persecution of the Jerusalem Christians. Little is told of Paul's second stay at Corinth, save that it lasted for three months, and that the Jews plotted to kill him when he was expected to sail from Corinth for Syria.

His stay there, however, was made memorable by the letter which he wrote to the Church at Rome. Rome had long been the goal of his desires. "I must see Rome," had been his ruling passion for some tune. But one event after another had prevented him from carrying out this ambition, so he writes to them the famous letter, in which he makes plain the way of salvation. This letter has well been called the Constitution of the Church and the Letter to the Galatians, perhaps written during this same period at Corinth, the Magna Charta of the Church. The Letter to the Galatians lays down the great principle of salvation by faith, and not by works, whereas the Letter to the Romans shows the great steps and principles of the plan of salvation. The letter was probably sent to Rome by Phoebe, a pious woman in the church at Cenchrea, which was near Corinth, and whom Paul commends to the Roman Christians as a "succourer of many, and of myself also." We can think of her boarding the vessel at Cenchrea, bound for Rome, with the precious manuscript hidden somewhere about her person. Through the fidelity and toil and loyalty of such messengers as these, the letters of St. Paul reached those for whom they were intended. If the age-long preservation of these letters is a fact which excites our wonder and merits our gratitude, hardly less so does the fact of their safe dispatch from one part of the world to another by messengers such as Phoebe, the deaconness of Cenchrea.

After three months' stay in the house of his convert, Gaius, at Corinth, Paul prepared to sail from Corinth to Syria, where he would celebrate the Passover. After that, his plan was to go to Rome, and from Rome to Spain, the rich and powerful province far to the west. But just before the ship sailed, Paul received a warning that there was a plot among the Jews to kill him. The ship would be filled with Jews going up to the feast, and their plan evidently was to throw Paul overboard when the ship had reached the high seas. Warned of this by some faithful and humble Christian friend, Paul abandoned this voyage and went by land through Macedonia to Thessalonica and Philippi. Luke was now with him. His other companions, Sopater of Berea, Aristarchus and Secundus of Thessalonica, Gaius of Derbe, Timothy, Tychicus and Trophimus, had gone ahead as far as Troas, where they waited for Paul and Timothy. After a tedious five days' journey from Neapolis, the port of Philippi, to Troas, Paul and Luke joined the others at that place and there remained seven days.

A MEMORABLE MEETING

In Luke's account of this visit at Troas, we have a reference to the Christian custom of breaking bread on the first day of the week, our Lord's Day. Paul was planning to depart from Corinth on Monday morning, and not knowing when he should see these Trojan Christians again, he tarried long with them at the celebration of the Supper, and then discoursed with them at great length about the mystery of Christ. The upper chamber was probably a large room in the high tenement house of Carpus, where Paul afterwards tells us that he left his cloak behind him. Night had come and there were lights in the room where the company were gathered together.

Imagination likes to dwell on that scene. No doubt, the night was warm and the air was close, made more so by the sputtering candles and ill-smelling lamps. In a central position stands, or sits, St. Paul, earnestly declaring unto them the word of Life, and in his own face and on his frail body the marks of suffering from the hardships through which he had passed since first he came to Troas. Near him is Luke, the beloved physician; and not far away, Timothy, dearest of his friends; and near Timothy, Titus; and grouped near them, the other members of his traveling missionary band, Gaius, Secundus, Aristarchus, Sopater, Trophimus and Tychicus. The company is made up of not many wise, not many rich, not many noble, but the hard working humble people of the port of Troas, listening eagerly and intently to their great master and teacher as he unfolds to them the riches of Jesus Christ.

At the open window sits a young man named Eutychus. Weary from the labors of yesterday, and overcome with the close air, Eutychus fell into a deep sleep as Paul was long preaching, and losing his balance, pitched from the window on the third story, to the pavement below. His friends rushed down and took him up, supposing him to be dead. But when Paul came down, he embraced him and said, "Trouble not yourselves, for his life is in him." He had him carried upstairs again, and then went on with his interrupted sermon, until the sun made his appearance over the distant Aegean. When Paul departed, the young man had recovered consciousness, and his parents and friends were greatly comforted concerning him.

All of Paul's companions embarked on a vessel which was to stop at Assos, about twenty miles distant. But Paul chose to go by land. The crowded quarters of a little ship pitching on the Egeian afforded little opportunity for retirement, prayer and meditation. Paul, who had prepared himself for his ministry with three years' retirement in Arabia, and afterwards at Tarsus, feels now a special need of quiet, solitude, self-examination, retrospection and anticipation. When he had set out from Ephesus to go into Macedonia and Greece, be had great plans, after a visit to Jerusalem, to turn again toward the west, visiting Rome, and from Rome to Spain. But now be seems to be in doubt as to his future. He has premonitions of trouble, trials, and danger and persecution. Yet, as Christ set His face steadfastly toward Jerusalem, so Paul is determined, in spite of warnings from without and misgivings from within, to press on to Jerusalem. He goes, as he said a little later to the elders of the Church at Ephesus, "Bound in the Spirit to Jerusalem, not knowing the things that shall befall me there, save that the Holy Ghost witnesseth in every city, saying that bonds and afflictions abide me." Walking that day, through the oak groves that bordered the sea, all by himself, Paul was preparing to drink his cup and lift his cross.

Assos, when Paul saw it on this trip, was a city of no little splendor, with a great theater and a citadel which dominated the sea and land for many a mile. Here the ship took Paul on board and proceeded to Mitylene. The vessel was proceeding by one day stages along the coast of Asia Minor, sailing by day and lying to at night. During the day, commencing with the early morning, the wind in the Aegean comes from the north and toward sunset, the soft south winds begin to blow. Therefore the favorable time for sailing was by day. Mitylene was a town on the island of Lesbos, the home of the celebrated Grecian poet, Sappho. In this town where "burning Sappho loved and sung" Paul and his companions spent the night, and those who loitered near the waterfront, or sailors in their ships at anchor in the harbor, heard them singing sweeter songs than those of Sappho, the songs of souls reborn.

Another day's sail brought them to Chios, now known as Scio. Thus to this island where Homer was born came the world wanderer who was writing the great Iliad and Odyssey of Christian faith and hope. Homer's hero after the fall of Troy wandered over the world, buffeted by wind and sea, meeting with strange adventures, before he came home again to his rocky Ithaca. Through the genius of Homer, his wanderings have found an echo in multitudes of hearts in every age and generation since. But the wanderings of St. Paul brought light to them that sat in darkness and in the shadow of death and awakened in their hearts the sweet music of redeeming grace.

A MEETING AT MILETUS

The next day the ship anchored off Trogyllium, a town on the end of a promontory jutting out into the sea and opposite the island of Samos. Paul's visit is still recalled there by the name given to an anchorage, St. Paul's Port. Hoisting sail again the next morning, in a few hours they reached Miletus. Miletus was forty miles south of Ephesus and had been a city of some renown. It was noted as the birthplace of the philosophers, Thales, Anaximander, and Democritus. At Miletus, on a future visit, Paul left one of his companions, Trophimus, sick. It was not Paul's purpose to make a visit to Ephesus, for he was hurrying forward so as to get to Jerusalem by the Feast of Pentecost. But when he found himself only forty miles from the city tender memories awoke in his heart and he yearned to see his friends once more. While the ship lay in the harbor, taking on and discharging cargo, he sent a messenger to Ephesus and summoned the elders of the Church to come to him at Miletus. Somewhere in a vacant spot along the shore of the harbor, and after the sun had set in the west, they had their prayer-meeting and exchanged their farewells. On this occasion, feeling that he would never see their faces again, Paul delivered a beautiful farewell address, which, as much as anything he ever said or wrote, lets us into his heart and constitutes the greatest statement ever made on the duties, responsibilities, privileges and joys of the Christian ministry. He spoke as follows:

"Ye know from the first day that I came into Asia after what manner I have been with you at all seasons, serving the Lord with all humility of mind, and with many tears and temptations, which befell me by the lying in wait of the Jews; and how I kept back nothing that was profitable unto you but have shewed you, and have taught you publicly, and from house to house, testifying both to the Jews and also to the Greeks, repentance toward God and faith toward our Lord Jesus Christ. And now, behold, I go bound in the spirit unto Jerusalem, not knowing the things that shall befall me there: Save that the Holy Ghost witnesseth in every city, saying that bonds and afflictions abide me. But none of these things move me, neither count I my life dear unto myself, so that I might finish my course with joy, and the ministry, which I have received of the Lord Jesus, to testify the gospel of the grace of God. And now, behold, I know that ye all, among whom I have gone preaching the kingdom of God, shall see my face no more. Wherefore I take you to record this day, that I am pure from the blood of all men. For I have not shunned to declare unto you all the counsel of God. Take heed therefore unto yourselves, and to all the flock, over the which the Holy Ghost hath made you overseers, to feed the church of God, which he hath purchased with his own blood. For I know this, that after my departing shall grievous wolves enter in among you, not sparing the flock. Also of your own selves shall men arise, speaking perverse things, to draw away disciples after them. Therefore watch, and remember, that by the space of three years I ceased not to warn every one night and day with tears. And now, brethren, I commend you to God, and to the word of his grace, which is able to build you up, and to give you an inheritance among all them which are sanctified. I have coveted no man's silver, or gold, or apparel. Yea, ye yourselves know, that these hands have ministered unto my necessities, and to them that were with me. I have shewed you all things, how that so laboring ye ought to support the weak, and to remember

the words of the Lord Jesus, how he said, It is more blessed to give
than to receive."

A FAREWELL MESSAGE

Happy indeed, is every minister who at the conclusion of his
ministry in any city or at any church can make a similar testimony.
Industry, courage, fearlessness, tenderness of appeal, warning and
admonition, all these were represented in Paul's ministry at Ephesus. It is interesting and affecting to take what Paul says in this
farewell address about his not counting his life dear unto himself
so that he might finish his course with joy, and place it alongside
his farewell message to the world, in the last part of his Second
Letter to Timothy, "I have fought a good fight, I have finished my
course, I have kept the faith." Like his Master, for the joy set
before him, he despised the shame and endured the cross.

This Miletus speech of Paul is notable also because it preserves
for us an otherwise lost, but very precious, saying of Christ, for
Paul concluded his address by saying, "I have shewed you all
things how that so laboring, ye ought to support the weak and to
remember the words of the Lord Jesus, how he said, It is more
blessed to give to receive." There were many sayings in
which Christ taught this lesson and many beautiful ways, even the
supreme way of the Cross, in which He illustrated its truth; but as
a distinct and special utterance of Christ, this is the only record we
have of it. It was a fitting conclusion to a great speech, and read by
us today, constitutes a noble eulogy on the life and ministry of St.
Paul. In spite of all his labors, trials, shipwrecks, bonds and imprisonment, he discovered what every follower of Paul and Christ
discovers, how it is more blessed to give than to receive.

When he had concluded his address, Paul kneeled down with
the elders from Ephesus and his own friends from the ship and
prayed with them all. When he rose from his knees to go back to
the ship, every cheek was wet with tears of sorrow, and as they
kissed him farewell they sorrowed most of all at the prospect of
never seeing his face again. Always somewhere on the shores of
life's sea, the best of friends must part, and always, it gives the
inward pain of parting; nor is the pain less intense when Christian
friends part. Christian faith does not obliterate the landmarks of

affection's empire, nor does it disannul the tender emotions of the heart, but rather adds to their intensity and poignancy. Yet, when Christian friends part, they have the hope of meeting again in that better country where they no more go out and come in. We doubt not that as these Ephesian friends, with the tears falling fast down their cheeks, took their affectionate farewell of Paul, he reminded them of that better country, the heavenly, where partings are no more.

The next stop of the ship was at Coos, a run of about six hours. Coos was once noted as the home of the medical school of Aesculapius. After leaving Coos, the ship rounded the promontory of Cnidus, and so came to the island of Rhodes and into the harbor of the city of Rhodes. Here they saw the two legs, all that remained of the famous Colossus of Rhodes. This enormous image was an idol of the god of the Sun, Apollo, and also served as a lighthouse for shipping in that part of the Mediterranean. The Colossus, 105 feet high, bestrode the entrance to the harbor of Rhodes, and in its day of splendor ships sailed between its legs. Long before Paul's visit to Rhodes, the Colossus had been destroyed by an earthquake. God uttered His voice: the earth shook, and one of the seven wonders of the world came down in ruins. We wonder if Paul saw in the ruins of the great image of the Sun god, a prophecy of what the Gospel would do to idolatry throughout the world. However formidable and impregnable the strongholds of Satan then may have seemed to Paul and his companions, within four centuries the worship of idols in heathen temples, by the edict of the Roman Emperor himself, was outlawed.

TRAVELING TO TYRE

At Patara, Paul and his companions left the small vessel in which they had been coasting along the shore of Asia Minor and took passage in a larger ship, probably one of the Alexandria grain ships which was in the trade between Alexandria, in Egypt, and Italy. Because of the prevailing winds and sea, the towns on the southern shore of Asia Minor were half-way stopping places for ships making the run from Alexandria to Italy. On his next voyage, as we shall see, his voyage to Rome, Paul's ship came from Cae-

sarea to Myra, not far from Patara and there the centurion trans-
ferred its prisoners to an Alexandria grain ship bound for Italy.
Taking advantage of the prevailing west wind, the new ship in
which Paul was traveling made a straight run for it to Tyre on the
coast of Syria. On the way, they sighted the Island of Cyprus, and
as Paul viewed its rugged mountains rising out of the sea, and
perhaps saw some of the white buildings of Paphos, he recalled,
no doubt, his trip through Cyprus with Barnabas and Mark on the
first missionary journey.

Tyre was an ancient Phoenician city, whose king, Hiram, had
assisted David in the building of the temple at Jerusalem. It was a
famous and prosperous maritime city in Old Testament times,
and from Tyre mariners had gone out into all parts of the Mediterranean world to found their colonies, the most notable of which
was Carthage, founded in the ninth century B.C. But when Paul
visited Tyre its empire and glory had long since departed. One of
the most striking fulfillments of Old Testament prophecies has
been the fate of Tyre. Predicting the overthrow and destruction of
this proud city "at the entry of the sea," and which said of herself,
"I am perfect in beauty," Ezekiel said: "Behold, I am against thee,
O Tyre, and will cause many nations to come up against thee as
the sea causes its waves to come up; and they shall destroy the
walls of Tyre and break down her towers; I will also scrape her
dust from her and make her a bare rock. She shall be a place for
the spreading of nets in the midst of the sea. I have spoken this,
saith the Lord Jehovah, and she shall become a spoil of the nation."

The principal part of the city was, for purposes of safety, built
on a rocky island near the mainland. Besieged and partly conquered by Nebuchadnezzar of Babylon, and brought into subjection
to Babylon, in 332 B.C., Tyre was besieged by Alexander the Great.
After a memorable siege of seven months, Alexander took and
destroyed the island citadel by building a causeway from the mainland across the narrow strait. Today, ancient Tyre, once the site of
splendid temples, palaces and towers, is nothing but barren rocks,
against which, with melancholy reverberation, as if repeating the
judgments of the Lord, break the waves of the Mediterranean; and
on those rocks, just as Ezekiel predicted, the fishermen today
spread their nets.

As the ship was discharging cargo at Tyre and would remain for some days, Paul went on land and sought out the Christian disciples of the town. There in pleasant fellowship with them he tarried for seven days, telling them as he had told the Ephesian elders at Miletus, that "bound of the Spirit," he was on his way up to Jerusalem. When the ship was ready to sail, the whole company of the Christian disciples at Tyre, men, women, and little children, accompanied Paul down to the shore, where they all kneeled together, and with the wind from the Mediterranean breathing a gentle benediction, Paul commended them to the love and care of God.

JOURNEYING ON TO JERUSALEM

Running down the Syrian Coast, the vessel touched next at Ptolemais, where it remained for one day, and where Paul met with the disciples. Ptolemais is the site of the Acre of the Crusades, and where, in 1799, Napoleon was repulsed by the Turks. Paul and Napoleon! What a contrast! The one in prison in Rome for the sake of Christ and the salvation of the world; the other in prison at St. Helena because the safety of the world demanded it; the one with the recollection of those in every city and country to whom he had brought the tidings of hope and light eternal through Jesus Christ; the other with the recollection of thousands who had fallen in battle in every land to further his ambitions; the one from his prison at Rome, sending out messages which throbbed with love and affection for his friends in distant parts of the world; the other, on his rock dungeon in the mid-Atlantic, as the end approached, wondering if there was a single soul in the world who loved him.

The journey from Ptolemais to Caesarea is a short one, and probably was made by land. At Caesarea Paul was entertained in the house of Philip the Evangelist, one of the original seven deacons. The two men, Paul and Philip, had much in common, for it was Philip who had evangelized the despised Samaritans and had baptized the Ethiopian eunuch on his way home to the empire of Queen Candace. As a colleague and close friend of the first Stephen, Philip must have recalled to Paul painful memories of the part he took in the stoning of Stephen. Yet both men must have wondered at the marvelous grace of God. Here they were, brothers in Jesus Christ, seated together in the home of Philip, the once head and front of the cruel persecution of the disciples at Jerusalem, the man who breathed out slaughter with every exhalation, and the evangelist and deacon who had been the friend and companion of the martyred Stephen. God works in a mysterious way His wonders to perform.

While Paul was at Caesarea, there came down from Jerusalem a prophet named Agabus, the same who at Antioch had stood up and signified by the Spirit that there was to be a great famine over all the world during the reign of Claudius. Under the guise of a symbol, Agabus now prophesied Paul's arrest by the Jews and his deliverance to the Romans. Loosing Paul's girdle, he took it, and having bound with it his own hands and feet, said, "Thus saith the Holy Ghost, So shall the Jews at Jerusalem bind the man that owneth this girdle, and shall deliver him unto the hands of the Gentiles." On hearing this prediction, the companions of Paul begged him not to go up to Jerusalem. But Paul, although deeply sensitive to their tender interest and solicitude for him, was not to be moved. He replied, "What mean ye to weep and to break my heart, for I am ready not to be bound only, but also to die at Jerusalem for the name of the Lord Jesus." When they saw his mind in the matter, they ceased from trying to persuade him, and sadly, but with acquiescence, said, "The will of the Lord be done." Paul then departed with his companions and some of the disciples at Caesarea for Jerusalem, taking with him Mnason, one of the first converts in the island of Cyprus, and a man of some property, who had a house at Jerusalem where Paul was to lodge.

What thoughts were in the mind of Paul as he saw again, and for the last time, the familiar panorama of the Holy City? Did his mind run back to that day of the long ago, when, as a young enthusiast for the traditions and hopes of Israel, he had come up from Tarsus to sit at the feet of the great doctor of the law, Gamaliel? How much had transpired since then—his persecution of the Church, his conversion on the way to Damascus, his three years in Arabia, his visit with Peter at Jerusalem, his long years of waiting at Tarsus, the call of Barnabas to Antioch, the first missionary journey to Cyprus and to Galatia, the second journey through Asia Minor and across the sea into Europe; through Macedonia to Athens and Corinth, then back to Antioch; the third journey with its long stay, great triumphs, and desperate peril at Ephesus; the second visit to Macedonia and to Greece, and then the long sea voyage to Caesarea. All this had taken place since Paul first saw the Temple of Herod flaming in the Syrian sun. From what he said to the weeping friends from whom he parted at Miletus, Tyre and Caesarea, we know that Paul entered Jerusalem with the full and solemn conviction that his missionary labors were nearing an end, and that before long he would be bound for the Lord's sake.

14

MOBBED AT JERUSALEM

On the first day after his arrival in Jerusalem, Paul and his companions met with James, the brother of the Lord, who was the leader of the Church at Jerusalem, and with the elders of the Church. With him he brought the offering for the poor which had been collected in Greece, Macedonia, Asia, Phrygia and Galatia. He gave them a full account of his labors among the Gentiles and what things God had wrought through his ministry. When they heard these things they were glad and glorified God. But there was a cloud on the horizon. Wherever Paul had gone he had aroused the enmity of the Jews. Many of the Jews from Ephesus, Thessalonica, Athens and Corinth were then in Jerusalem in attendance upon the feast. These men had slandered Paul, telling the multitude of Jewish converts in Jerusalem that Paul, wherever he went in the Gentile world, taught the Jews to forsake Moses, not to circumcise their children, nor to pay the slightest attention to ancient and sacred Hebrew customs.

This was not the truth. What Paul contended for was the freedom of the Gentile Christians, that to become a Christian, it was necessary for a Gentile to be circumcised and become a Jew. As for the Jewish converts, Paul took the position that they were free or not, as they pleased, to observe the Jewish laws and customs. Paul himself had not abandoned all of those customs; he had taken the Nazarite vow at Cenchrea and now had come to Jerusalem to attend the Passover. But the false report that he openly taught the Jewish converts to abandon all Jewish customs had poisoned the minds of the Jewish Christians in Jerusalem against him. James and the leaders of the Church were concerned lest this prejudice and misunderstanding with regard to Paul should hinder the work of the Church in Jerusalem, indeed, that it should jeopardize the life of Paul himself.

AN EXTRAORDINARY VOW

They, therefore, made Paul a rather extraordinary proposal. In brief, it was this: there were four men in Jerusalem who had taken the Nazarite vow on them. In that day it was the custom for pious and well-disposed Jews to assist men who had taken the Nazarite vow. The sacrifices which had to be offered at the close of the period of the vow involved no little expense, and it was considered a charitable act to have a part in those expenses. The argument was that when even the most intense Hebrew Christians in Jerusalem saw Paul in the temple under a vow and assisting those who had taken the vow, their prejudice and enmity toward Paul would abate. It would be a testimony to them and to all the Jews at Jerusalem that Paul had been falsely charged with disrespect for Jewish laws and customs, and that he walked circumspectly and observed the law.

The proposition must have been most distasteful to Paul, for in carrying out the plan, he ran some risk of seeming to withdraw from the firm position he had taken as to the way of salvation, that men are saved through faith in Christ, and not through any rites or works of the law; and there is little reason to doubt that it was not only a solicitude about Paul's safety and the progress of the Gospel at Jerusalem, but an intense Jewish feeling on the part of James and others at Jerusalem which led to the proposal. But Paul was the man who would be "all things to all men" if he could save some. He had a passionate longing for the salvation of his own people, and no doubt it often grieved and pained him to think that his own personality was one of the chief obstacles in the way of the Jews receiving the Gospel. He would go to great length in disabusing their minds of false prejudice concerning himself.

It must have been with this thought in mind that Paul submitted to the proposal of James and the elders of the Church. He went into the Temple enclosure with the four men who were under a vow and went through all the prescribed rites and observances. But on the last of the seven days of purification and observance in the Temple an event occurred which destroyed altogether the effect of Paul's condescension and generosity. Among the multitude who thronged the Temple enclosure were Jews from Asia, some of them, no doubt, members of the mob who had stirred up the people against him at Ephesus. Some days before, they had seen Paul on the streets of Jerusalem in the company of Trophimus, one of his Ephesian converts, and a Gentile. When they saw Paul in the Temple enclosure, they either believed, or pretended to believe, that he had brought Trophimus into the Temple with him. Thereupon, they set up a great cry, "Men of Israel! Help! this is the man who teacheth all men everywhere against the people and the law of this place, and further brought Greeks also into the Temple and has polluted this Holy Place!"

SAVED BY THE SOLDIERS

Nothing was so calculated to stir up the frenzy and passion of the Jews as the charge that a Jew had brought a Gentile into the Temple area. Soon the entire city in the vicinity of the Temple was in an uproar. Seizing upon Paul, the leaders of the mob dragged him out of the Temple and shut the doors behind him. In the outer area of the Temple the mob commenced to beat Paul and soon would have made an end of him, had not the Roman soldiers appeared on the scene. Because of the frequent outbreaks of the turbulent populace at Jerusalem, a guard of Roman soldiers had been stationed in the Tower of Antonia at one corner of the Temple area. Sentinels stationed in the Tower heard the uproar and saw the tumult and hurried to the captain, Lysias, who, without a moment's delay, summoned his guard and hurried down among the mob. The moment the mob saw the chief captain and the soldiers, they stopped beating Paul, and he was delivered out of their hands. The chief captain tried to find out who Paul was and what he had done, but the screams of the enraged Jews were so loud and incessant that he was not able to discover the cause of the uproar. He therefore had Paul hand-cuffed to two soldiers and carried up the stairs to the Tower. As soon as the soldiers turned with Paul in their custody to ascend the stairs, the baffled mob, like so many wild beasts, rushed after them, and, but for the courage of the soldiers, would have torn Paul out of their hands.

Before he was put in the prison in the Tower, Paul addressed himself at a favorable moment to the chief captain, saying to him, "May I speak unto thee?" Lysias was surprised to be accosted in the Greek tongue, for, as his answer to Paul showed, he supposed that he was an Egyptian adventurer who had recently been giving the Romans trouble by stirring up the Jews against them. This man had given himself out to be a prophet and collected in the desert some thousands of men whom he persuaded to follow him to the Mount of Olives, promising them that they would see the walls of Jerusalem fall down at his command. He had been routed and his army dispersed by the governor, Felix, but he himself had escaped with many of his followers. Amazed no doubt to be taken for such an agitator and rebel, Paul quickly gave an account of himself as to his race and nation, saying, "I am a man who am a Jew of Tarsus, a city of Cilicia, a citizen of no mean city, and I beseech thee suffer me to speak unto the people."

A MESSAGE TO THE MULTITUDE

Never was Paul in a more dramatic circumstance and never did he appear to greater advantage. Back of Paul was the frowning fortress of Antonia. Gathered around him and underneath him on the stone stairway were the centurions and the legionaries, with their shields and their spears raised aloft to keep back the mob which howled and raged in the courtyard below. But the moment Paul, stretching forth his hand with that familiar gesture which had been witnessed by the peasants of Galatia and the philosophers of Mars Hill, commenced to speak, a deep hush fell over the multitude, the stern Roman legionaries rested on their weapons, and the raging mob ceased from their cries and lowered their clenched fists. In his speech Paul spoke as follows:

"Brothers and fathers, listen to the defense I now make before you. I am a Jew, born at Tarsus in Cilicia, but brought up in this city, educated at the feet of Gamaliel in all the strictness of our ancestral Law, ardent for God as you all are today. I have persecuted this Way of religion to the death, chaining and imprisoning both men and women, as the high priest and all the council of

elders can testify. It was from them that I got letters to the brotherhood at Damascus and then journeyed thither to bind those
who had gathered there and bring them back to Jerusalem for
punishment. Now as I neared Damascus on my journey, suddenly
about noon a brilliant light from heaven flashed round me. I
dropped to the earth and heard a voice saying to me, 'Saul, Saul,
why do you persecute me?' 'Who are you?' I asked. He said to me,
'I am Jesus the Nazarene, and you are persecuting me.' (My companions saw the light but did not hear the voice of him who talked
to me.) I said, 'What am I to do?' And the Lord said to me, 'Get
up and make your way into Damascus; there you shall be told all
you are destined to do.' As I could not see owing to the dazzling
glare of that light, my companions took my hand and so I reached
Damascus. Then a certain Ananias, a devout man in the Law, who
had a good reputation among all the Jewish inhabitants, came to
me and standing beside me said, 'Saul, my brother, regain your
sight!' The same moment I regained my sight and looked up at
him. Then he said:

"'The God of our fathers has appointed you to know his will, to
see the Just One, and to hear him speak with his own lips.

"'For you are to be a witness for him before all men, a witness
of what you have seen and heard.

"'And now, why do you wait? Get up and be baptized and wash
away your sins, invoking his name.'

"When I returned to Jerusalem, it happened that while I was
praying in the temple I fell into a trance and saw him saying to
me, 'Make haste, leave Jerusalem quickly, for they will not accept
your evidence about me.'

"'But, Lord,' I said, 'they surely know it was I who imprisoned
and flogged those who believed in you throughout the synagogues,
and that I stood and approved when the blood of your martyr
Stephen was being shed, taking charge of the clothes of his murderers!'

"But he said to me, 'Go; I will send you afar to the Gentiles—'"

The mob heard him in silence as he gave an account of his early
days, his zeal for the law, his conversion, and how in the Temple
he had a vision of Christ who told him to go and preach the
Gospel unto the Gentiles. It was Paul's relationship with the Gentiles which roused the passions of the Hebrew mob, and at the

mention of the Gentiles they again lifted up their voices and roared, "Away with such a fellow from the earth! It is not fit that he should live!" The execration and hatred of their speech was accompanied by furious and wild gesticulations, tearing off their clothes and throwing dust and stones into the air.

Seeing that his life was in danger from such a mob, the chief captain had him brought into the tower and ordered him to be scourged, hoping in this way to find out the truth about Paul. But as they were fastening Paul to the whipping post, Paul said to the centurion who had charge of the scourging, "Is it lawful for you to scourge a man that is a Roman and uncondemned?" Startled at his question, and knowing how serious an offense it was to scourge a Roman, and a man who was uncondemned, the centurion reported what Paul had said to his superior, the chief captain, saying to him, "Take heed what thou doest. This man is a Roman." Thereupon, the chief captain came at once to Paul and said, "Tell me, art thou a Roman?" When Paul said that he was, the captain, still incredulous, said, "With a great sum I obtained his freedom." Men of great wealth frequently purchased Roman citizenship. But Paul said, no doubt with a degree of pride, "But I was freeborn." Immediately the chief captain ordered him loosed from his bonds and treated him in a far different manner.

PAUL AGAIN BEFORE THE SANHEDRIN

The next day, determined to know the truth, he had Paul brought before the Sanhedrin. There, in the presence of the high priest, Paul commenced his defense. Twenty years had passed since Paul had stood before the Sanhedrin. How different the circumstances now. Then, he appeared before the Sanhedrin in order to secure letters from them authorizing him to arrest and persecute the Christians of Damascus. Now, he appeared before them as an ambassador of Christ.

He commenced his defense by saying, "Men and brethren, I have lived in all good conscience before God until this day." Even in his pre-Christian days, Paul had been conscientious in what he had done. The last thing, however, in Paul's mind would have been to claim non-responsibility for his actions, because he did them conscientiously. On the contrary, he distinctly says in one of his letters that for this false and wicked conduct of his pre-Christian days he obtained mercy through the goodness of God. His reference here in this instance before the Sanhedrin to his good conscience, undoubtedly had to do with his relationship to Israel. He means that as a faithful member of the Jewish commonwealth and nation he has nothing to reproach himself with. This opening sentence so enraged the high priest, Ananias, that he commanded one of those who stood near Paul to smite him on the mouth. To smite a man on the mouth was a sign of unusual detestation of what the man had spoken. At the trial of Christ before the high priest, one of the officers who stood by struck Jesus with the palm of his hand, saying, "Answerest thou the high priest so?" On that occasion Jesus answered, with majestic self-control, "If I have spoken evil, bear witness of the evil; but if well, why smitest thou me?" But now it was the disciple and not the Master who was on trial. Stung by the insult, and hurt by the injustice of it, Paul blazed forth with this scorching rejoinder to the high priest, "God shall smite thee, thou whited wall! For sittest thou to judge me after the law, and commandest me to be smitten contrary to the law?"

Some of those who stood by him, reproached him saying, "Revilest thou God's high priest?" Whereupon Paul answered, "I wist not, brethren, that he was the high priest, for it is written, 'Thou shalt not speak evil of the ruler of thy people.'" Some have taken this sentence of Paul to mean that he really did not know that he was talking to the high priest; and from the fact that he did not know that he was addressing the high priest, it has been inferred that Paul's thorn in the flesh was a weakness of the eyes. The delightful author of *Rab and His Friends*, Dr. John Brown, in an essay on Paul's Thorn in the Flesh takes this view of the case. It is difficult, however, so to interpret the answer of Paul, for he knew that the one who had commanded him to be smitten was his judge, and he reproached him for his injustice. The more likely thing is that after his anger had died down and his attention had been called to his remarks to the high priest, Paul said, "Brethren, I wist not that he was the high priest," that is, "I did not remember to whom I was speaking."

Convinced that he had no chance for a fair trial before such a jury, Paul resorted to a clever device to save his life. In passing judgment upon the course he took, we must remember that the first law of life is self-preservation. Paul knew that part of the Sanhedrin was made up of Sadducees and the other part of Pharisees, the two factions holding irreconcilable views as to the resurrection. So he cried out, "Men and brethren! I am a Pharisee, the son of a Pharisee. Of the hope and resurrection of the dead I am called in question." Strictly speaking, that was not so; the chief complaint of the Jews was not that he preached the resurrection of the body, but that he proclaimed the resurrection of Jesus as a proof of His Messiahship.

DISCORD AND DISPUTE

But the apple of discord which Paul had flung out into the Sanhedrin at once did its work, and there arose an angry dispute between the Pharisees and the Sadducees, the Sadducees disbelieving in resurrection, angel or spirit; the Pharisees believing in all of them. Those who were Pharisees, thinking that Paul was the champion of their doctrine, cried out, "We find no evil in this man. But if a spirit or an angel hath spoken to him, let us not fight against God." The Sadducees, on the other hand, clamored against him as a blasphemer and demanded his life. In the angry contest between the two parties, Paul was about to have been pulled in pieces, and the chief captain, who had been a haughty witness to the whole performance, ordered his soldiers to go down and take Paul back to the castle. That night, Paul had one of those four visions which came to him in the great crises of his life. The first was at Jerusalem when he was told that the people of Jerusalem would not listen to his preaching and that he must go hence unto the Gentiles. The second came when his life was in danger in Corinth. The third, on the evening of this stormy day before the Sanhedrin, and the fourth in the midst of the shipwreck on the Mediterranean. The Lord stood by him and said, "Be of good cheer, Paul, for as thou hast testified for me in Jerusalem, so must thou bear witness also at Rome." It was comfort, and yet not comfort. There was no assurance of deliverance from bonds and imprisonment, but only the assurance that his life would be spared at Jerusalem. He must witness for Christ at Rome.

Baffled in their efforts to get Paul's life when they attacked him in the Temple enclosure, on the stairs of Antonia's castle, and now before the Sanhedrin, forty or more of the most bitter of the Jews joined in a conspiracy and bound themselves together under a curse, saying that they would neither eat nor drink until they had killed Paul. The plot was to have the Scribes and Pharisees request the chief captain, Lysias, to bring Paul down to the Sanhedrin for a second hearing on the morrow. While he was coming down, they would pull out their knives and kill him.

The news of the wicked plot leaked out and word of it reached Paul's nephew. He was a quick thinking lad and at once went to the castle where he was permitted to see Paul. When he told Paul of the plot, Paul, although always ready to be offered up, and yet always determined to guard his life to the utmost, called one of the centurions and requested him to take his nephew to the chief captain. When he came to the chief captain, that officer took him aside privately and asked him what he had to say. He then told him of the plot and besought the chief captain not to yield to the request of the Scribes and Pharisees to bring Paul down to the Sanhedrin. With a parting admonition to him to say nothing of what had passed between them, the chief captain dismissed Paul's nephew, and calling two trusted centurions, ordered them to make ready at once two hundred soldiers to go to Caesarea, together with seventy horsemen and two hundred spearmen. They were to be ready to march that night at the third hour. At nine o'clock, and with great secrecy, Paul was taken out of his prison, seated on one of the animals, and the cavalcade started at once for Caesarea. That same night they reached the town of Antipatris. Here the foot soldiers, feeling that Paul was now reasonably safe, returned to Jerusalem and the horsemen went on with Paul to Caesarea, twenty-six miles northwest of Antipatris.

15

MAKING FELIX TREMBLE

Caesarea was the seat of the Roman administration of Judea and the residence of the governor, Felix. The purpose of the captain of the guard, Lysias, in sending Paul down to Felix was to save him from outrage and assassination at the hands of his enemy, and also to pass on to Felix what Lysias thought to be a difficult case. When Paul had been brought before the governor, one of the centurions handed Felix the letter which had been sent down by the chief captain Lysias, and which read as follows:

"Claudius Lysias, to his excellency the governor Felix: greeting. This man had been seized by the Jews and was on the point of being murdered by them, when I came on them with the troops and rescued him, as I had ascertained that he was a Roman citizen. Anxious to find out why they accused him, I took him down to their Sanhedrin, where I found he was accused of matters relating to their law, but not impeached for any crime that deserved death or imprisonment. I am informed a plot is to be laid against him, so I am sending him to you at once, telling his accusers that they must impeach him before you. Farewell."

After inquiring of Paul what his province was, and learning that he was from the neighboring province of Cilicia, Felix said, "I will hear thee when thine accusers also come." In the meantime, he ordered him to be imprisoned in Herod's judgment hall.

Paul did not have long to wait for his accusers, for after five days, Ananias and the elders from Jerusalem come down with a special lawyer, or pleader, named Tertullus. When the case was called Paul was brought in from his dungeon and Tertullus made the following speech:

"Your excellency," he said to Felix, "as it is owing to you that we enjoy unbroken peace, and as it is owing to your wise care that the state of this nation has been improved in every way and everywhere, we acknowledge all this with profound gratitude. I have no wish to weary you, but I beg of you to grant us in your courtesy a brief hearing. The fact is, we have found this man is a perfect pest; he stirs up sedition among the Jews all over the world and he is a ringleader of the Nazarene sect.

"He actually tried to desecrate the temple, but we got hold of him. Examine him for yourself and you will be able to find out about all these charges of ours against him."

The speech of Tertullus was a typical lawyer's plea. It included the usual flattery and mock deference to the judge on the bench. In brief, Tertullus charged Paul with being a ringleader of the sect of the Nazarenes, an instigator of sedition among the Jews throughout all the world, and one who had profaned the Temple. He said that the Jews themselves would have legally tried Paul had not the chief captain, Lysias, come down upon them and with great violence taken him out of their jurisdiction.

PAUL'S DEFENSE

Paul now was given his opportunity to make his defense. This he did in a straightforward and effective manner. After courteous words of introduction in which he expressed his satisfaction that he was to state his case before a judge and governor who had long familiarity with the Jewish people and their customs, Paul said:

"As I know you have administered justice in this nation for a number of years, I feel encouraged to make my defense, because it is not more than twelve days, as you can easily ascertain, since I went up to worship at Jerusalem. They never found me arguing with any one in the temple or causing a riot either in the synagogues or in the city; they cannot furnish you with any proof of their present charges against me. I certainly admit to you that I worship our fathers' God according to the methods of what they call a 'sect'; but I believe all that is written in the Law and in the prophets, and I cherish the same hope in God as they accept, namely that there is to be a resurrection of the just and the unjust. Hence I too endeavor to have a clear conscience before God and men all the time. After a lapse of several years I came up with alms and offerings for my nation, and it was in presenting these that I was found within the temple. I was ceremonially pure, I was not mixed up in any mob or riot; no, the trouble was caused by some Jews from Asia, who ought to have been here before you with any charge they may have against me. Failing them, let these men yonder tell what fault they found with my appearance before the Sanhedrin!—unless it was with the single sentence I uttered, when I stood and said, 'It is for the resurrection of the dead that I am on my trial today before you.'"

Paul denied every charge made against him. He had not stirred up the people; neither had he profaned the Temple, and as for his being a heretic, he says he believes all things which were written in the law and in the prophets. His visit to Jerusalem was prompted by the highest motive—to bring alms to his suffering people. The Asiatic Jews who assaulted him in the Temple found him engaged in no act of violence or sacrilege; but since this charge had been made against him that he had profaned the Temple and stirred up a riot, he demanded that the Asiatic Jews who had commenced the thing ought to be present and substantiate their charge if they could.

PAUL BEFORE FELIX

Having heard the prosecutor and the defendant, Felix reserved judgment, saying that when the chief captain Lysias came down he would make a further examination into the case. Paul was remanded to his prison in the old palace of Herod the Great, but with a degree of liberty which was very unusual. He was to suffer no hardship and such of his acquaintances as desired to see him were to have free access to his prison. So far, Felix had done well. The leniency which he showed to St. Paul was evidence that he was greatly impressed by the prisoner and by what he had said. This is still further shown by the fact that after three days Felix sent for Paul and asked him to discourse concerning the Gospel before him and his wife Drusilla.

Paul before Felix and Drusilla is another of those overwhelming contrasts in which the Bible abounds. On the throne sat Felix, the procurator, a faded and withered pagan. Formerly a slave who had risen to his high office as the favorite of the Emperor Claudius, his rule as the governor of Judea had been marked by injustice and violence. Greed, cruelty and lust were stamped upon his face. At his side sat the lovely Jewess, Drusilla, a daughter of Herod Agrippa. She had been married first of all to a Gentile, who for her sake became a Jew, and then, with the aid of a sorcerer, she had been won from her husband to become the paramour of Felix. All that was shameful and dishonorable in humanity was represented by Felix and Drusilla as they sat on their throne awaiting the sermon by Paul. Before them, with chains on his arms, and his body scarred with the marks of his witness for Christ, perhaps shading his eyes with his hands so that the bright light would not hurt them, his coarse garments, which he had woven with his own hands, contrasting sharply with the velvet and purple of Felix and his paramour, stood the lonely ambassador for Christ. Paul was now face to face with one of his great opportunities, and nobly did he embrace it. Recently his public utterances had been in defense of his own conduct and to save his own life. Now, he was glad to take up his cherished theme, "Christ and Him Crucified."

As he stood before them he reasoned of righteousness and temperance and judgment to come. It was a great service that was held that day in the procurator's palace at Caesarea. No processionals, no preludes, no anthems, and a congregation of just two persons. Yet what a service and what a sermon! The sated Roman was expecting that Paul would have something to say about the distinction between Christianity and Judaism, or upon the subject of predestination, or perchance the resurrection of the dead; and the brilliant Drusilla was hoping to hear something of a new cult, or a new philosophy, or some new interpretation of the Old Testament. They were looking for an hour's entertainment, but Paul gave them judgment and searching of heart.

Paul could preach a great doctrinal sermon when he wanted to, but he could also preach an ethical sermon when it suited the occasion, yet an ethical sermon, a sermon on conduct, based on the great redemptive facts of the Christian faith. He was not unfamiliar with the lives and characters of those who sat on the throne before him, and he preached a sermon that was eminently and painfully practical. Instead of flattering his aristecratic hearers, or avoiding any subjects which might have been interpreted as having a personal application, Paul reasoned with them of righteousness, temperance, and judgment to come.

The administration of Felix had been full of dishonesty, extortion and injustice, and Paul discoursed of righteousness, justice; how God would not overlook the acts of wicked injustice and would regard the cry of the poor and the oppressed and surely avenge them, and how righteousness and judgment are the habitation of His throne. Paul mentioned no places, repeated no names, gave no dates, but his sermon covered the past life of Felix. The Governor thought of the bribes he had paid or received; of the innocent men he had falsely charged and cast into prison; of the crowds of people in the street upon whom he had loosed his cruel soldiery; of the homes that had been laid waste and made desolate at his command. When he did these acts, he had no compunction of conscience, but now, under the preaching of Paul, that terrible past rose before him in fearful resurrection and accusation.

As Paul reasoned of self-control, temperance, chastity, Felix thought of those sins, common among high class Romans of that day, but of which today it would be a shame even to speak. And here Drusilla, too, began to show some uneasiness. She thought of her own shameful escapades; of the lover she had deceived, of the husband she had abandoned, and now her adulterous union with Felix. Perhaps she thought, being a Jewess, that Paul would have something to say about the new faith of the Nazarenes in its relationship to Judaism. But instead of that, he preached an old fashioned Hebrew sermon on the Seventh Commandment.

By the time Paul had reached the third head of his sermon, both Felix and Drusilla were very unhappy and both anxious for the preacher to come to a close. Paul in his preaching did not leave out, as so many do, the territory of life to come. He preached not only to the times, but to the eternities. His preaching had the power of the world to come in it. Like the preaching of Christ, who ever spoke as standing under the rule of another world, Paul told Felix and Drusilla that this life is not all; that a man might have his good clothes, his good times, his mistresses, chariots and villas, and yet be cast into hell in the next world;

and that all three of them, Paul, Felix and Drusilla, must stand before the judgment seat of Christ and give an account of the deeds done in the body.

PAUL PREACHES— FELIX TREMBLES

No wonder Felix trembled. Never did preaching have a greater vindication or a preacher receive a greater tribute than when Felix, the hardened, withered, licentious despot, trembled. He was the last man in in the world one would have expected to tremble. He had listened in his day to all sorts of orators and enthusiasts and philosophers, yet, of them all, this Jewish prisoner was the only one who had ever made him tremble. The Word of God as used by St. Paul that day was quick and powerful, sharper than any two-edged sword, piercing even to the dividing asunder of joints and marrow, a discerner of the thoughts and intents of the heart. Felix could break up the meeting and dismiss the preacher, but it was some time before he could still the storm of conscience that had arisen within his heart. Paul had started the bell to tolling, and Felix could not muffle it. Wherever he went, this preacher went with him. If to the baths, the scented waters and costly unguents could not soothe the troubled mind; if he sat in the Emperor's box at the theater or at the circus, above the cries of the gladiators and the shouts of the populace, he heard a still small voice reasoning of righteousness, temperance and judgment to come. Or did he drive his chariot along the sea wall, out of the sea there arose to confront him an awful throne of judgment.

This sermon, like so many others, made a deep impression, but had little result. The preacher had brought Felix to the gates of the great opportunity. The voices of those within were crying to him, "Come in, come in, eternal glory thou shalt win." But Felix would not go in. Felix trembled, but he would not go in. He might have been a brand plucked from the burning. With all his crimes and wickedness, the blood of Christ could have made him a fit citizen of the City of the Redeemed; but he would not go in. God said, "Today," but Felix said, "Tomorrow," and tomorrow never came. He dismissed the preacher, saying to him, "When I have a convenient season I shall call for thee." Luke tells us that he sent Paul back to prison, keeping him there with the hope that Paul's friends would raise a sum of money for his ransom.

During the two years Paul was a prisoner in Herod's Palace, Felix often sent for him and had him preach to him. It was a strange case of a wicked man wanting to hear a fearless preacher, just as Herod feared John, and brought him frequently out of the dungeon, so that he might hear him preach, knowing that he was a righteous man.

16

ALMOST PERSUADING AGRIPPA

After Paul had been in prison for two years at Caesarea, during which period the curtain drops on his life, Felix was succeeded by a new governor, Porcius Festus. Festus was a much higher type of man than Felix and made a real effort to administer justice. One of the most difficult cases which he found confronting him was that of St. Paul. Luke says that he left Paul in the dungeon because he was anxious to please the Jews, but it is clear from what followed that Festus did not contemplate injustice toward the Apostle. Three days after his arrival at the seat of his procuratorship, Caesarea, Festus went up to Jerusalem. There, the chief of the Jews and the high priest appeared before him and requested that he bring Paul up from Caesarea to Jerusalem for trial. Their plan was to have him assassinated in the course of the journey. Festus was not misled, and told the Jews that Paul would remain at Caesarea, to which he himself would return in a few days. If they had anything to charge against Paul, they could go down there and prosecute the case before him. From what Festus said afterwards to Agrippa, it seems that the Jews wanted Paul sentenced without a trial, for he says, "To whom I answered, It is not the custom of the Romans to deliver any man to death before that he which is accused have the accusers face to face, and have license to answer for himself concerning the crime laid against him."

After ten days, Festus returned to Caesarea, and the very next day took his place on the judgment seat and commanded Paul to be brought in. The Jews who had come down from Jerusalem repeated the charges against Paul which had been made by their advocate, Tertullus, when he prosecuted the case before Felix. Paul again made his defense, denying the three charges, that he had profaned the Temple, violated the laws of the Jews, or raised sedition against Caesar. Festus was evidently impressed with his prisoner; but desiring to go a considerable distance in placating his unruly subjects, the Jews, he asked Paul if he was willing to go to Jerusalem and there be judged in the procurator's court, for just as Pilate did in the case of Jesus, the procurator frequently held court at Jerusalem.

Realizing the grave dangers of a journey to Jerusalem, and of a trial in that city, Paul stood on his right as a Roman citizen and appealed to the supreme court of the world, Caesar's judgment seat, saying, "I stand at Caesar's judgment seat, where I ought to be judged. To the Jews, have I done no wrong, as thou very well knowest." It was clear that Paul had violated no laws of the Jewish people. His position is, that if he is to be tried on the other counts, that of stirring up sedition and doing things contrary to Caesar, he ought to be tried at the court of Caesar himself. There is a mingling of high self-respect and dignity with deep and tender pathos in what Paul said in his appeal to Caesar, "For if I be an offender, or have committed anything worthy of death, I refuse not to die. But if there be none of these things whereof these accuse me, no man may deliver me unto them. I appeal unto Caesar." What he means to say is, that if he were guilty, he would plead guilty, and there would be no difficulty about his trial or his sentence. He would accept death as the just wages of his transgression. But since he is innocent, and has done nothing worthy of death, he will not permit himself to be delivered unto his enemies.

Somewhat amazed at this bold appeal, yet knowing that Paul was a Roman citizen, and that as a citizen he had a right of appeal, Festus asked him if his decision was final. "Hast thou appealed unto Caesar?" When Paul repeated his declaration, the procurator answered, "Unto Caesar thou shalt go." Paul chose; but it was God's plan that he should stand before Caesar. While Festus was waiting for the sailing of a convenient ship upon which he could place Paul and other prisoners, King Agrippa and his sister Bernice, came down to Caesarea to pay their respects to the new governor. Agrippa was the last of the Herods, but not King of Judea, for Judea had no king since Herod the Great. It was ruled by procurators, subject to the authority of the legate of Syria, resident at Antioch. Agrippa, the great-grandson of Herod the Great, was permitted by the Romans to rule over small portions of the territory of Judea in much the same manner that the Indian princes of a later day were permitted to exercise a little authority under British rule in India. His office was largely titular, and he himself a mere agent of Rome in that section of the country where he was called King. Agrippa was the brother of Drusilla, the paramour of Felix. The other sister was Bernice, who appears with Agrippa at the palace of Festus and listened to the preaching of Paul. The constant close relationship between Bernice and Agrippa was the occasion of no little scandal, and such relationship in high circles was no unheard of thing in that day and generation.

Because of Agrippa's familiarity with Jewish history and customs, Festus availed himself of the opportunity to discuss with Agrippa the case of Paul, how he had found him in prison when he succeeded Felix in the procuratorship, how he had refused to condemn him and give him over to the Romans without a trial, and when the trial was finally held, how nothing was brought against Paul showing him to be worthy of death, and how the whole thing seemed to be a dispute about certain superstitions of the Jews and concerning one Jesus, which was dead, whom Paul affirmed to be alive. Since there was no evidence to convict Paul of transgression against the Roman law, and since Paul refused to go up to Jerusalem and plead his case before the Jewish Council, and had appealed unto Caesar, there was nothing for him now to do but to send him forward to Rome. When he heard about the case, Agrippa told Festus that he would like to hear the man speak for himself, and his words indicate that he had heard a great deal about Paul and the Gospel which he preached. Festus at once set the next day for the hearing.

With great pomp and magnificence, followed by their court and retainers, Agrippa and Bernice came to the palace of Festus, where were gathered the aristocracy and the military of the city. The rich gold and scarlet garments, and the glittering shields and spears of the legionaries, as they ranged themselves about the hall, made a brave and dazzling show. At a nod from Festus,

Paul was brought into the chamber. His long imprisonment had intensified the pallor of his thin and worn face. His self-spun garments contrasted strangely with the rich silk and velvets of the royal party.

We can imagine the craning of necks and the whispering as Paul took his stand before the dais. This hearing before Agrippa was not in the nature of a trial. Agrippa had no judicial function, and Paul had already made his appeal to Caesar. The whole thing was staged as a sort of entertainment for Agrippa and his sister Bernice. With the two soldiers to whom he was chained standing on either side of him, their rugged warlike forms sharply contrasting with the emaciated prisoner between them, Paul waited for a word from Festus permitting him to speak. Festus, addressing himself to King Agrippa and Bernice, and all who were present, said, "Ye see this man about whom all the multitude of the Jews have dealt with me both at Jerusalem and also here, crying that he ought not to live any longer. But when I found that he had committed nothing worthy of death, and that he himself had appealed to Augustus, I have determined to send him, of whom I have no certain thing to write of to my lord. Wherefore, I have brought him forth before you, and especially before thee, O King Agrippa, that after examination had, I might have somewhat to write. For it seemeth to me unreasonable to send a prisoner, and not withal to signify the crimes laid against him."

Addressing Agrippa

From what Festus said in introducing Paul to Agrippa and to the assembly, it seems that he was puzzled as to just what report he should send to Caesar when he dispatched Paul to Rome. The difficulty was that Paul apparently was not guilty of any transgression against the Roman law, yet he had made his appeal to the judgment seat of Caesar and to that court he must be sent. When Festus had finished his introduction, Agrippa greeted Paul kindly, saying to him, "Thou art permitted to speak for thyself." Then Paul stretched forth his hand with that familiar gesture which we see now for the last time, and commenced what, in many ways, was the greatest speech of his career.

"I consider myself fortunate, King Agrippa, in being able to defend

myself today before you against all that the Jews charge me with; for
you are well acquainted with all Jewish customs and questions.

"Pray listen to me then with patience.

"How I lived from my youth up among my own nation and at
Jerusalem, all that early career of mine; is known to all the Jews.
They know me of old. They know, if they choose to admit it, that as
a Pharisee I lived by the principles of the strictest party in our
religion. Today I am standing my trial for hoping in the promise
made by God to our fathers, a promise which our twelve tribes
hope to gain by serving God earnestly both night and day. And I am
actually impeached by Jews for this hope, O king! I once believed it
my duty indeed actively to oppose the name of Jesus the Nazarene.
I did so in Jerusalem. I shut up many of the saints in prison, armed
with authority from the high priests; when they were put to death, I
voted against them; there was not a synagogue where I did not often
punish them and force them to blaspheme; and in my frantic fury I
persecuted them even to foreign towns.

"I was traveling to Damascus on this business, with authority
and a commission from the high priests, when at midday on the
road, O king, I saw a light from heaven, more dazzling than the
sun, flash round me and my fellow travelers. We all fell to the
ground, and I heard a voice saying to me in Hebrew, 'Saul, Saul,
why do you persecute me? You hurt yourself by kicking at the
goad.' 'Who are you?' I asked. And the Lord said, 'I am Jesus, and
you are persecuting me. Now get up and stand on your feet, for I
have appeared to you in order to appoint you to my service as a
witness to what you have seen and to the visions you shall have of
me. I will rescue you from the people and also from the Gentiles—to whom I send you, that their eyes may be opened and that
they may turn from darkness to light, from the power of Satan to
God, to get remission of their sins and an inheritance among
those who are consecrated by faith in me.' Upon this, O King
Agrippa, I did not disobey the heavenly vision; I announced to
those at Damascus and at Jerusalem in the first instance, then all
over the land of Judea, and also to the Gentiles, that they were to
repent and turn to God by acting up to their repentance. This is
why the Jews seized me in the temple and tried to assassinate me.
To this day I have had the help of God in standing, as I now do, to
testify alike to low and high, never uttering a single syllable be-

yond what the prophets and Moses predicted was to take place. Why should you consider it incredible that God raises the dead, that the Christ is capable of suffering, and that He should be the first to rise from the dead and bring the message of light to the people and to the Gentiles?"

The two things which Paul emphasized in his speech were the fact of his miraculous conversion and his preaching of the doctrines of the resurrection, and especially the doctrine of the resurrection of Christ. Agrippa and Festus heard him with interest and patience until he came to speak of the suffering and resurrection of Christ, and how through Christ, a great light dawned for the people and for the nations. There Festus interrupted him with a loud exclamation—"Paul, thou art beside thyself! Much learning doth make thee mad!" The speech had been addressed chiefly to Agrippa, but it was Festus who now interrupted Paul telling him that he was beside himself. Although clearly friendly to Paul, Festus had the Roman disdain for Hebrew history and prophecies, and this strange tale of a vision and a voice on the Damascus highway, and the resurrection of One who had been crucified—all this, to the Roman procurator, was sheer nonsense. He thought Paul was a visionary, overcome with his own enthusiasm. Paul, at least, was earnest enough in his preaching to have men think him mad. This is a charge which could never be laid against many preachers.

Paul courteously and firmly denied that he was excited or unbalanced in mind, saying, "I am not mad, most noble Festus, but speak forth the words of truth and soberness." Then he appealed to King Agrippa, who was familiar with Hebrew history and had heard of the alleged facts about this Jesus, for, Paul said, "this thing was not done in a corner." Before Agrippa could make an answer or commit himself in any way, Paul cried to him, "King Agrippa, belivest thou the prophets? I know that thou believest." Paul was certain that whatever acquaintance Agrippa had with the prophets, that acquaintance was such as would give him the greatest respect for their moral and spiritual teaching and for their predictions as to the future. Paul was making his appeal to those great moral intuitions and convictions to which every preacher can address himself, and concerning which he can say to the hearer, or ever the hearer can answer for himself, "I know that thou believest!

AGRIPPA ALMOST PERSUADED

In the face of Paul's appeal, Agrippa refused to commit himself, and said to Paul, so that all about him heard, "Almost, thou persuadest me to be a Christian!" His answer seems to have been a mixture of satire and friendly sympathy, as if he had said to Paul, "Paul, thou art an earnest, sincere man, and thou hast suffered great things in behalf of the Gospel which you preach; but surely, you do not imagine that in a single speech you are going to make a Christian out of me!"

Had we been present in the hall of Festus when Agrippa pronounced his now famous sentence, we would have known just what he meant, whether he was speaking seriously or in jest. But whatever he meant to say, Paul took him at his word, and lifting up his manacled arms cried out in a great and dramatic climax to one of the greatest speeches ever delivered, "I would to God, that not only thou, but also all that hear me this day, were both almost, and altogether such as I am, except these bonds." Noble, self-forgetting, soul-seeking Paul. Agrippa, Festus, Bernice, the centurions, the legionaries, all the nobles of Caesarea, with all their sins, crimes and follies and superstitions—Paul would have them all to be saved, and to be reconciled to God. He would have no one wear a chain such as he was wearing; he would not want them to pass through the shipwrecks, the scourgings, the stonings, the prisons, the stocks, the loneliness, the weariness through which he had passed, and gladly, for the sake of Christ.

But if he had to choose between bonds and imprisonment with Christ, and freedom and wealth and purple raiment without Christ, he lets them know that he would choose Christ with bonds. It is as if Paul had said to Agrippa and all who were in the hall that day, "I would not have you to bear the stonings, the imprisonment, the shipwrecks, the revilings, the sufferings of my ministry for Christ. But my night hours of communion with God, my sense of the presence of Jesus Christ, even in the dungeon, my visions of God's glory and of the face of Jesus, my love for all men, my deep joy in seeing men changed and recreated by Christ, my sweet fellowship with humble disciples of Jesus throughout the world, the tokens of gratitude and love which I have received from my converts, my willingness to forget and to forgive injuries, my freedom from fear for today, and fear for tomorrow, my hopes for the future, my expectation to receive at length a crown of glory which passeth not away—all this, O King Agrippa, O Bernice, O most excellent Festus, I would that you possessed, all, all, save these chains!"

Deeply moved by the dramatic appeal of Paul, King Agrippa rose up from his seat, gave a sign that the audience was over and together with Festus and Bernice went out from the chamber. When they were by themselves, they talked about this strange prisoner, and the agreement between them was that Paul had done nothing worthy of death or of bonds, and Agrippa said that but for the fact that Paul had made his irrevocable appeal to Caesar, he might have been set at liberty. Back in his prison in the palace of Herod the Great, Paul, we can be sure, followed up that most earnest sermon with a prayer of supplication and intercession for Agrippa and those who heard him that day. He would remember, too, what Ananias had said to him when he came to see him as he lay blind and helpless after his conversion in the house in the street called Straight in Damascus, "Go thy way, for he is a Chosen Vessel unto me to bear my name before the Gentiles and kings and the children of Israel." Nobly had Paul acquitted himself and splendidly and faithfully had he borne the name of Jesus before King Agrippa and Festus the governor. Now he is to appear before earth's greatest potentate, and the presence of Caesar himself bear witness to the King of Kings.

17

SHIPWRECKED

A vessel of Adramyttium, a town in Asia Minor, was about to sail for its home port and the governor, Festus, took advantage of the sailing of this vessel to send Paul and other prisoners forward on the first leg of their journey to Rome. The prisoners were committed to the charge of a centurion, Julius, the captain of the Augustus Band. Paul had with him for his two companions, Luke, the beloved physician, and Aristarchus, whose home was at Thessalonica. It must have been with no little relief and satisfaction of mind that, after two years in prison, Paul found himself once again on the deck of a ship and on his way to Rome. The vessel on which he was traveling was probably a small coasting vessel, and it was evidently the plan of the centurion to sail first to some port in Asia Minor where he might find a larger ship sailing to Italy. In case he could not find such a vessel, he could go on through the Aegean Sea to Troas, and across to Philippi, and then by land over the Egnatian Way to Dyrrachium, and from there across the Adriatic Sea to Brundusium, and from that port up to Rome by the Appian Way.

The first stop of the vessel was at Sidon, a run of sixty-seven miles up the coast from Caesarea. On the way to Sidon the ship passed the port of Ptolemais and Tyre, where Paul had visited the Christian disciples two years before on his way up to Jerusalem, and where the disciples had tried to dissuade Paul from continuing on his journey. Sidon was one of the most ancient cities of the world. It was mentioned by Homer in the Iliad and Odyssey and was warred against by the Jews in the day of Joshua. In the vicinity of Sidon Elijah was ministered to by the widow of Zarephath, whose son he raised to life. Some of the inhabitants of Sidon followed in the footsteps of Jesus, and Jesus Himself visited the neighborhood of Sidon and forever immortalized it by the healing of the Syrophoenician woman's little daughter.

While the vessel took on or discharged cargo at this ancient Phoenician port, Paul was permitted by the centurion to land and refresh himself and have fellowship with the disciples who were in the city. The next day the ship sailed for Myra, on the south coast of Asia Minor. The direct route was to the south of Cyprus, but an contrary wind from the west compelled them to run to the northeast of Cyprus, "under Cyprus," as Luke says, and so through the sea of Cilicia and Pamphylia to Myra, a city of Lycia. Myra was a important port and in its commodious harbor there were vessels from all parts of the Mediterranean world. There the centurion found one of the Alexandria grain ships about to sail for Italy, and he embarked his prisoners and soldiers on this larger vessel.

In that day of crude navigation, ships did not take a direct course through the open sea as they do today. Thus it was that this grain ship from Alexadria, in Egypt, was found in a port of Asia Minor. Instead of running directly across to Italy through the Mediterranean, it first beat its way northward to this port in Asia, and thence would proceed by short runs to Italy. Egypt was the granary of Rome, and these famous grain ships of Alexandria constituted the bread line of the Roman Empire. The ships were not infrequently in the imperial services, and special privileges were granted to their mariners. From the fact that this ship was not only heavily laden with wheat, but carried two hundred and seventy-six passengers and sailors, we know that it must have been a vessel of considerable dimensions, certainly, not far behind some of the large sailing vessels which still ply the seven seas.

One of the Latin historians, Lucian, describes a vessel similar to that on which Paul took passage. The length of the ship was one hundred and eighty feet, its breadth, forty-five feet, and its depth over forty feet. It had one lofty mast and a great square sail of flame color. The ship stood high out of the water at the bow and the stern and bore in glittering letters the name of a heathen

goddess on either side of the bow. Because of the storms and
waves which the vessel on which Paul sailed survived, we judge
that it must have been decked over, at least in part.

SLOW SAILING

The west wind still prevailing, the vessel made slow headway,
and after many days had proceeded only as far as Cnidus, at the
entrance to the Aegean Sea. Unable to make headway into the
Aegean, the wind being from the west and the north, the master
of the ship took a course to the south which brought him under
the lee of Crete, that is, to the south of that island. When they had
rounded the Cape of Salmone, at the extreme eastern part of the
island, they sailed along the southern coast as far as Fair Havens,
an open roadstead near the town of Lasea. So much time had been
consumed already on the voyage, that the period for safe navigation in the Mediterranea was almost over. Realizing this, Paul,
although he was a prisoner, warned the centurion that it would be
dangerous to proceed further at that time of the year and that they
should winter where they were. This was not the advice of a
novice, a land lubber, but one who had great experience in sailing,
for Paul tells us he had suffered shipwreck three times before this
last voyage to Italy. "Thrice," he says, "have I suffered shipwreck,
a night and a day have I been in the deep." The captain of the ship
and the owner of the ship were both intent on proceeding further
and scornfully dismissed the counsel of the Hebrew prisoner. The
centurion, who was in command of the vessel, not unnaturally
paid more attention to what the master and the supercargo had to
say, and as soon as the wind began to blow softly out of the south,
they hoisted anchor with the purpose of sailing along the coast as
far as Phenice.

The officers thought that they could undertake without peril
the short journey of about twenty miles from Fair Havens to
Phenice. But the ship was barely under way in the open sea,
when the wind suddenly shifted from the south to the north, and
the roaring gale, called by the navigators Euroclydon, struck the
ship and drove her twenty-three miles out of her course, where
she took refuge from the hurricane under the lee of the little
island of Clauda, protected somewhat there from the fury of the

gale by the high mountains. The sailors first of all hoisted on board the water-logged long-boat which they had been towing. Then they had resort to an ancient device of navigators, what is called" frapping" the ship, that is, undergirding the ship with ropes and cables to keep her timbers from parting beneath the assault of the angry waves. They then furled the great square mainsail, and with only a storm sail to steady the vessel, let her drive before the wind and sea.

All through the night the ship drifted toward the south, and when morning dawned, fearful lest the vessel should founder, they lightened her by casting overboard some of the cargo, and on the next day threw overboard part of the heavy tackling and gear of the ship, which was thrashing about over the vessel before the fury of the winds and waves, endangering the lives of the passengers and interfering with the handling of the ship. The one peril which they now feared was that they should drift upon the Syrtis, shifting reefs of sand in the Gulf of Sidra, off the north coast of Africa. Their one hope was to keep the vessel in the open sea and drift toward the west.

During these days of the raging of the storm, the heavens were so overcast that the mariners could see neither sun nor stars and were unable to take any reckoning as to their course. Every one had given up hope of being saved. We can imagine what a dismal company it must have been, the two hundred and seventy-six passengers, soldiers, prisoners, officers and sailors, tossed about by the violent plunging of the vessel, drenched with the sea which swept over her; without food or drink, and unable to do anything but cling to rope or spar or rail, and wait for what seemed to be certain destruction.

PAUL'S SHIPBOARD SPEECH

Then it was that Paul stood forth in their midst and said:

"Sirs, ye should have hearkened unto me, and not have loosed from Crete, and to have gained this harm and loss. And now I exhort you to be of good cheer: for there shall be no loss of any man's life among you, but of the ship. For there stood by me this night the angel of God, whose I am, and whom I serve, saying, Fear not, Paul: thou must be brought before Caesar: and, lo, God hath given thee all them that sail with thee. Wherefore, sirs, be of good cheer: for I believe God, that it shall be even as it was told me. Howbeit we must be cast upon a certain island."

Hope had died in every breast but one. The centurion, the master of the ship, the supercargo, had tried all the devices of ancient navigation. The sailors, soldiers and passengers and prisoners had done all that they could to keep the ship from sinking or driving on the rocks. The heathen had invoked all their gods to save them from an ocean grave. The net result of all their efforts and commands and prayers was despair. All hope that they should be saved was taken away. Then it was that faith achieved one of her greatest victories. The Hebrew prisoner stood forth in the midst of the panic-stricken, despairing company, and lifting up his voice so that it could be heard above the roar of the wind and the pounding of the waves, told his fellow-voyagers to be of good courage and put their trust in God. His confidence was based not merely on the fact that God had appeared to him in a vision in the prison at Jerusalem, and had told him that he must stand before Caesar, but was born out of another vision which God had granted to him in the midst of the storm, assuring him that he would be brought before Caesar, and that although the ship would be wrecked on a certain island, all who sailed with him would escape with their lives.

In the ultimate crisis the man of faith, as always, was the man of influence and the man of authority. Never did Paul preach a greater sermon or under more dramatic circumstances than when he stood up on the deck of this storm-driven, water-logged craft and said that even in the storm he belonged to God and would serve Him, "Whose I am, and whom I serve."

Day after day, night after night passed by, and still no sun shone, no kindly stars appeared, and the slowly foundering vessel was driven up and down at the mercy of winds and waves. But suddenly, on the fourteenth night, the ship's company heard the watchman at the prow of the vessel cry out, "Breakers ahead!" Luke says that the "shipmen deemed that they drew near to some country." The only way in which they could know this was either through the ominous reverberation of the waves breaking on a rockbound coast, or by seeing through the night the white foam where sea and land met.

It was with a mingling of joy and fear that the passengers heard the cry, "Breakers ahead!" Joy, because land anywhere, under any circumstances, lighted for them a candle of hope after the terrible two weeks at sea; fear, because they realized the danger of the ship breaking up on the rocky shore. The sailors at once took soundings and found it to be twenty fathoms; after a little, they sounded again and found it to be fifteen fathoms, one hundred and five feet. Soundings taken by the British Admiralty in the vicinity of the shore where Paul is supposed to have been wrecked confirm the soundings which are recorded by Luke in his graphic and marvelously accurate account. The rapidly diminishing depth of the sea let them know that they were in close proximity to shore. Indeed, without the soundings, the noise of the waves breaking against the stern precipices of the island must have let them know that they were close to land. Fearful lest the vessel should strike in the night, they let four anchors down from the stern, and, in the beautiful language of St. Luke, "wished for the day." The reason the anchors were let down from the stern of the vessel, and not from the bow, was that with wind and tide toward shore, the vessel, if anchored at the bow, would swing her own length and that of the cables and run the risk of grounding.

The sailors now considered that their condition, so far as the ship was concerned, was hopeless. But since they were so close to land, there was a possibility of launching the long-boat and gaining the shore in that way. Under the pretense of lowering another anchor from the bow of the ship, they were letting down the boat and had it already in the water and were preparing to descend into it and desert the ship, when Paul, with his quick understanding, saw the danger, and summoning the centurion, said to him and to the soldiers, "Except these abide in the ship, you cannot be saved."

SAVED ON SHIPBOARD

A few nights before, Paul had assured the centurion that the whole ship's company would be saved, although the vessel would be destroyed. Here he tells him that unless the sailors are kept on the ship, none of the ship's company can be saved. There was no inconsistency or contradiction in this second declaration. Paul believed that God would save the ship's company as He had promised, but he also believed that God works through man's effort and free will. Thus, even in this thrilling shipwreck in the Mediterraean, we have an interesting illustration of the great truth to which Paul gave such eloquent utterance and explanation, the sovereign decree and invincible purpose of God in our salvation, together with man's free will and choice of eternal life. The centurion at once appreciated what Paul said, and ordered his soldiers to cut the rope attached to the boat, which soon drifted off into darkness.

When the morning dawned they were able to discern, through the gray mists the outlines of the land, and hope once more beat high in their hearts. During the fourteen days of the storm, the ship's company had been able to take little or no nourishment. Paul knew that they needed strength for the final effort which was before them and so encouraged them to take food, saying to them, "This day is the fourteenth day that ye have tarried and continued fasting, having taken nothing; wherefore, I pray you to take some meat; for this is for your health, for there shall not a hair fall from the head of any of you." Then lifting up his hand to heaven, and with officers, prisoners, soldiers and passengers reverently attending, and, no doubt, in their hearts, and each after his own tongue, joining in the prayer, Paul gave thanks to God in the presence of them all and began to eat. They followed his good example, with the result that every one was strengthened and encouraged.

With renewed strength they now turned to the task of throwing the cargo of wheat overboard. This had been partly done when the storm broke over them off Clauda, but only in part, as some of the wheat was needed for ballast. But now, in order to get over the rocks and the bars between them and the shore, they wanted the vessel to ride as light as possible, and for this reason, the wheat was thrown into the sea. They could see in the distance a place on the shore where a little creek emptied itself into the sea, and this seemed to be a favorable place for beaching the ship. They therefore hoisted the anchors, set the great mainsail, and let the ship drive toward the shore. They had made considerable progress when the ship grounded on a bar over which the waves were breaking. In a few minutes, with the violence of the great waves, the stern of the vessel began to break up, and it was necessary at once, if they had any hope to be saved, to quit the ship.

A strange index to the cruelty and brutality of the age is afforded in the record of Luke, who was one of the passengers, that as soon as the ship struck, the soldiers, realizing that they were responsible for the prisoners, drew their swords and were about to put them to death. But the centurion, Julius, for the sake of Paul, for whom he had now conceived a great admiration, if for no other reason, commanded them to refrain from their contemplated butchery. He then gave orders for every one to leave the ship, every man for himself. This they were not loath to do, and some by swimming, some hanging to planks or spars of the ship, they all escaped safely to the shore. "And so then it came to pass, they all escaped safe to land." The promise that God had given Paul in the midst of the storm had been wonderfully fulfilled.

STUNG BY A VIPER

The natives of the island who were living near the bay where the ship grounded, had witnessed the wreck and hurried down to the shore to do what they could for the comfort of the survivors. Luke calls them the "barbarians," not with any note of scorn or contempt, but because he wrote as a Greek, and the ordinary word to describe non-Greeks was barbarians. The people of this island, which the survivors of the wreck soon learned was Melita, or the modern Malta, were of Phoenician origin and race. A great bonfire was quickly kindled, for a cold rain was falling and those who had escaped from the wreck were drenched by the sea and exhausted by their final labors. Paul did not disdain to help in the task of gathering sticks for the fire. As he was casting an armful of fagots down by the fire, a viper which had coiled up for his winter's sleep, brought to life by the heat, buried his fangs in the Apostle's arm. It may have been that Paul did not see the serpent, or seeing it, was not afraid, for he allowed it to hang upon his arm long enough for the natives to cry out in astonishment and fear. In the heathen mind serpents were associated with divinity and the supernatural. The natives took the serpent to be an agent of heaven, for they cried out as they saw the viper on Paul's arm, "No doubt this man is a murderer, whom though he has escaped the sea, yet justice suffereth not to live."

But when Paul shook the viper off into the fire, and instead of swelling or falling down dead, suddenly, felt no harm and went out for another armful of fagots, the natives changed their minds and said that he was a god. The barbarians had a very keen sense of justice and vengeance. They knew nothing about the Christ whom Paul served and very little about God. They knew gods, but not God. Yet, even in their unenlightened hearts, there was the instinct of retribution. The moment they saw the viper clinging to Paul's arm, they connected that fate with some evil in the life of Paul. The gods, they thought, were on this man's path. He had managed to evade them on the sea, but they would not be robbed of their victim, and the viper was to accomplish what the sea had failed to do. The barbarians were wrong, of course, as to Paul, but as to the great instinct of justice and retribution, they were not wrong. They believed what is true, that wrong-doing brings suffering, that punishment is as inseparable from crime as heat from the flame of the fire, and that though hand join in hand, the wicked shall not go unpunished.

The governor of the island, whose name was Publius, was not in the least behind the natives in his kindness and hospitality to the shipwrecked company, for he received them into his ample palace and there entertained them for three days until they were able to secure more permanent accommodations. The father of Publius was dangerously ill with dysentery, and Paul proved how it is wise not to be "forgetful to entertain strangers," for he entered into the sick man's room, and laying his hands upon him, healed him of his disease. The report of this miracle spread through the island, and from all quarters they brought their sick and afflicted to Paul, that he might heal them. Even a shipwrecked Christian ought to bring a blessing to the island upon which he has been cast. Luke tells us little of their stay on the island, except the events just referred to, and how the people "honored them with many honors" and heaped their hospitality upon them. Brief as the story is, it is a charming tale of elemental brotherhood and kindness, showing how even in that hard, pagan world, where man's inhumanity to man made countless thousands mourn, the heart of man still had nobler promptings and revealed itself in deeds of courtesy and kindness.

After a stay of three months on the island, during which Paul, no doubt, preached the Gospel and won disciples to Jesus, another grain ship of Alexandria touched at the near-by port and the centurion embarked his two hundred and seventy-six passengers on this ship, bound, as their own had been, for Italy. The sign of this ship and the name of it was Castor and Pollux, sons of Leda, and who, by the gift of Zeus, shared immortality with one another on alternate days. These brothers were regarded as the special protectors of distressed mariners. But so far as the two hundred and seventy-six who had come aboard from the ship-wrecked vessel, their confidence now must have been, not in Castor or Pollux, nor any of the ancient alleged protectors of mariners, but in the God of the Hebrew prisoner who sailed with them.

Sailing probably in February, with a favorable south wind, the vessel soon reached Syracuse, eighty miles distant. Syracuse was famous in history for its great struggle with Athens in the beginning of the fifth century B.C. The Greek army under Nicias was defeated and captured, and perished amid terrible sufferings in the quarries of Syracuse. After three days in the port of Syracuse, the vessel set a course for Rhegium, a town in Italy, opposite Messina.

From Rhegium the vessel made its way through the straits of Messina, past the volcano of Stromboli on the left, and into the open sea to the west of Italy, where it headed for Puteoli, one hundred and eighty miles to the north. Steering through the strait of Messina, the vessel passed between what were spoken of in the ancient world as Scylia and Charybdis, twin monsters personifying the dangers of navigation. The ancient legend, as reflected in the tale of the Odyssey, made Scylia a monster who lived in a cave near the sea and reached out and seized men from the decks of passing ships, while Charybdis was a whirlpool eddy which sucked down and belched out the sea three times a day.

REACHING PUTEOLI

With top sail unfurled, a privilege which belonged to the Alexandria grain ships alone of all the ships which sailed the seas, the ship on which Paul was traveling sailed into the lovely bay, now called Naples, and came to anchor off Puteoli. About twenty years after Paul sailed into this bay, the harmless-looking mountain, upon which, no doubt, his eyes rested, covered with vines and vegetation, opened its mouth and poured death and annihilation on all in the vicinity. Among those who perished was the wife of that Felix who trembled before the preaching of Paul. Hard by Puteoli was Baiae, a fashionable watering place for Roman society, and where two years before the arrival of Paul, Nero had tried to murder his mother Agrippina, by embarking her in a ship so constructed that it would fall apart when at sea. Agrippina saved herself by swimming, only to be stabbed to death at her villa at the Lucrine Lake. Near at hand to Puteoli, also, was Capreae, the modern Capri, where Tiberius Caesar, under whom Christ was crucified, ended his days amid terrible sufferings and remorse.

As Puteoli was a very important port, it was not strange that Paul soon discovered that there were disciples in the town, and when they learned who he was, they gathered about him and asked him to remain with them and give them instruction. The considerate centurion, Julius, gave his consent, and Paul was permitted to remain with the Christians at Puteoli for seven days. Bidding farewell to his friends at Puteoli, Paul at length set out with the caravan of prisoners and soldiers for Rome, a distance of one hundred and fifty miles. At the town of Capua the caravan struck the great highway called the Queen of Roads, the Appian Way, which ran from Rome southeastward to Brimdusium. Near the town of Terracina there was a canal route, and it is possible that Paul and the other prisoners were put aboard one of these canal boats. The Roman poet Horace has left us an interesting and amusing account of travel by the canal boat, telling of the rough language of the boatmen, the lazy mules, the stings of the mosquitoes and the chorus of the frogs. The town of Appii Forum, fifty miles from Rome, was at the end of one of the stages of the canal boat, a gathering-place of teamsters and hucksters, and where travelers spent the night.

ARRIVAL IN ROME

Here Paul had a pleasant surprise. During the week he remained at Puteoli, word had reached the Christian community at Rome that Paul was coming to the city. With fine courtesy, a group of disciples went out this long distance to Appii Forum to meet him and welcome him to Rome. A little further on was the town of Three Taverns, and there a second delegation met Paul.

Luke tells us that when Paul saw these friends coming to greet him, he thanked God and took courage. We gather from this that Paul was suffering from the natural reaction of the terrible physical and mental experiences through which he had just passed. His great ambition had been to preach Christ at Rome, "I must see Rome." It was his imperial desire to lift up the cross of the King of Kings in the world's capital. Now, he was nearing Rome; but he was coming in chains, to be tried in the court of the cruel despot, Nero. We need not think it strange if Paul was distraught and in low spirits as he walked along beneath the fierce Italian sun, chained to one of the Roman soldiers. But when he saw these Christians from Rome, first at Appii Forum, and then at the Three Taverns, and recognized among them, perhaps some old friends, Aquila and Priscilla, Amplias, Herodion, Andronicus, Junia, Mary—he thanked God, and although a prisoner and in chains, approached Rome a conqueror and more than conqueror.

When Julius with his band of soldiers and prisoners had reached the summit of the Alban hills, they could see Rome in the distance. Coming down the western slope of the hills, they began to cross the vast spaces of the Roman Campagua, brilliant with the flowers of the springtime. Soon, they passed over the plains where, at a day not far distant, the earth beneath their feet would be honeycombed with narrow subterranean passages where men would lay their dead in hope of the doctrine of the resurrection of the body as it fell from the lips of the Hebrew prisoner who that day marched toward Rome. As they drew nearer to the city, the road was filled with throngs of people, coming and going; farmers returning with empty carts from the market; soldiers starting for service in Greece, Egypt, Syria, or Mesopotamia; wealthy men carried in litters by their slaves, going home to their summer villas on the hills; chariots of generals, senators and proconsuls. A centurion with a gang of prisoners in his custody was a common enough sight in those days, and no one paid the slightest attention to Julius and the prisoners he brought with him.

After a little, they passed the colossal tombs of the great men of Rome. Then into the city, past temples, arches, baths, colonnades, and palaces whose gilded roofs flashed back the afternoon sun. Down they came into the famous Forum, and up the Capitoline

Hill to the barracks of the Praetorian guard, where Julius handed over his prisoners. "And so," writes Luke, "we came to Rome." The dream of one of those prisoners had come true: He had come to Rome. Yet, save among a few believers who knew who he was, his entry that day excited not a ripple of interest or comment in that great world called Rome. But that day saw Rome's greatest conqueror enter her gates. When the proud monuments of imperial splendor upon which this prisoner gazed as he passed through the city shall have been leveled with the dust, and under the dust, Rome's most conspicuous monument will be a temple dedicated to the worship of that Christ for whose sake this heroic prisoner had come to Rome to witness and to die.

18

THE AMBASSADOR IN CHAINS

Upon his arrival at Rome, Paul was permitted to live in his own hired house, but guarded by a soldier who was responsible for his person. The fact that Paul was able to pay the expenses of four men who had taken the Nazarite vow at Jerusalem, that Felix kept him in jail hoping to receive a bribe, and that at Rome he lived in his own hired house, makes it clear that Paul had considerable resources at his command. It could not have been his own money, for he distinctly says that he has suffered the loss of all things for the sake of Christ; but he may have had influential friends who stood ready to assist him with their money. Some of those friends or, perhaps, the Church at Rome, put at his disposal the hired house in which he lived for two years.

When three days had passed, Paul called together the leaders of the Jews at Rome and said to them:

"Brothers, although I have done nothing against the people or our ancestral customs, I was handed over to the Romans as a prisoner from Jerusalem. They meant to release me after examination, as I was innocent of any crime that deserved death. But the Jews objected, and so I was obliged to appeal to Caesar—not that I had any charge to bring against my own nation. This is my reason for asking to see you and have a word with you. I am wearing this chain because I share Israel's hope."

In this courteous and diplomatic address, Paul made it clear to the Jews that he was innocent of any crime or offense against the Jewish people or their customs, and that his appeal to Caesar and his journey to Rome was in his own self-defense, and not because he brought any accusation against his people of Israel. He maintained that he was in a sense a martyr to the great Messianic hope of the Jewish people, for he said, "For the Hope of Israel, I am bound with this chain." The Jews answered that they had received no letter from the authorities at Jerusalem concerning him, neither had any of the Jews who had come to Rome from Jerusalem spoken against him, but they had heard a great deal about "this sect" of the Galileans, or Christians, of which Paul was a leader, and they would like to know what he thought about them, and what their ideas were, because everywhere "this sect was spoken against." This prejudice against Christianity prevailed not only among the Jews, but also among the Romans.

TELLING THE TRUTH

On a set day, the Jewish leaders came to Paul's hired house and to them he set forth the truths of the Gospel, telling them as Christ had done with His disciples, out of the law of Moses and of the prophets, that Jesus was the Messiah. The result was what had happened in so many other places—and what still happens wherever the true Gospel is preached—some believed and some did not. When some of those present showed a great hostility to the message of the Gospel, Paul spoke up clearly and plainly, declaring his purpose to give the Gospel to the Gentiles, since it was rejected by the Jews. In defense of his course, and as a prediction of it, he quoted the words of the prophet Isaiah:

"It was an apt word that the Holy Spirit spoke by the prophet Isaiah to your fathers, when he said,

"'Go and tell this people, "You will hear and hear but never understand; you will see and see but never perceive."

"'For the heart of this people is obtuse, their ears are heavy of hearing, their eyes they have closed, lest they understand with their heart and turn again, and I cure them.

"'Be sure of this, then, that this salvation of God has been sent to the Gentiles; they will listen to it.'"

This conference with the Jews is the last time we see Paul in action. The Book of the Acts of the Apostles comes to an abrupt close with the statement that Paul lived for two years in his own hired house, receiving all who came unto him, "preaching the Kingdom of God and teaching those things which concern the Lord Jesus Christ with all confidence, no man forbidding him." This is a strange ending for a great history and a great biography. It may be that Luke planned to write a third treatise and give the last chapter in Paul's life; but if so, he was not permitted to carry out his plans; at least, we have no further record from St. Luke concerning his great friend and traveling companion. For the rest of the story we must depend upon passages in the letters which Paul wrote at Rome and upon ancient traditions.

There are frequent references to Paul's imprisonment and trials in the letters to the Colossians, the Ephesians, the Philippians and Philemon. There are also references in the Second Letter to Timothy and that to Titus. From these letters we learn that there were with Paul at Rome, if not at the same time, at different periods of his imprisonment, Luke, the "beloved physician," Timothy, his dearest friend, Epaphras, Mark, Tychicus, his old Ephesian friend, Epaphroditus, who had come with a gift from the Church at Philippi, and Aristarchus, and Onesiphorus, who was "not ashamed of his chains." Demas also is mentioned as one who had forsaken him, and last but not least, the fugitive slave, Onesimus, who is handed down to immortality in the beautiful one-chapter epistle to Philemon.

Of necessity, a long period of time would elapse between Paul's arrival in Rome and his hearing before the Emperor, for in addition to the usual postponements and delays of judicial procedure, the accusers of Paul had to come from the other end of the Roman world. From what Paul says in his letter to the Philippians, we gather that he had great success in preaching the Gospel and in making converts to Christ, although he was a prisoner and in chains, for he says:

"I would have you understand, my brothers, that my affairs have really tended to advance the Gospel; throughout the whole of the Praetorian guard, and everywhere else it is recognized that I am imprisoned on account of my connection with Christ, and my imprisonment has given the majority of the brotherhood greater confidence in the Lord to venture on speaking the word of God without being afraid."

The whole Praetorian guard, which may be likened to a crack regiment stationed at the palace of a modern king, and all their friends, knew of the celebrated prisoner in their midst who preached Christ and Him crucified. Paul has every confidence in his acquittal at his coming trial, for he writes to his Philippian friends, "I know that I shall abide and continue with you all for your furtherance and joy of faith; that your rejoicing may be more abundant in Jesus Christ for me by my coming to you again"; and he tells Philemon to prepare lodging for him at Colossae, saying, "But withal prepare me also a lodging; for I trust that through your prayers I shall be given unto you."

LETTERS FROM PRISON

Among the letters written by Paul when in prison at Rome are the Letter to the Ephesians and the Letter to the Colossians, both of them profound statements concerning the person of Christ, the way of Salvation, together with personal and practical exhortations to daily Christian living. Nor can we forget the brief Letter to Philemon. Among those who heard Paul preach and became followers of Jesus, was a youth, Onesimus, a slave, who, after robbing his master, Philemon, at Colosse, had run away. With deep consideration for Philemon and with tender love for Onesimus, Paul sends Onesimus back to his former master with the letter which appears in our Bible as the Epistle of Paul to Philemon. In this letter Paul speaks of Onesimus as "my child, whom I have begotten in my bonds," meaning that Onesimus had been converted by him at Rome.

Playing on the name Onesimus, which means helpful, Paul speaks of Onesimus as one who was once unprofitable to Philemon, but now is profitable both to him and to Paul, so that the name Onesimus is no longer a misnomer. Paul says that he would have liked to have kept Onesimus with him, for he was very useful in ministering to him in his bonds, but that he could not conscientiously do this, now that he knows that Onesimus was a runaway from the home of Philemon. But in sending back this fugitive slave, Paul pays a lovely tribute to the transforming power of the Gospel, and to the tender relationship which ought to exist between all believers in Christ, for he asks

Philemon to receive Onesimus back, not as a slave, but as more than a slave, "a brother beloved," dear to both Paul and Philemon, "in the flesh and in the Lord." If Onesimus has robbed Philemon, Paul undertakes to make good the sum which had been taken—"I, Paul, will repay it." With an expression of the confidence that Philemon will do even more than Paul has asked, Paul tells him to prepare a lodging for him, since he hopes soon to visit him.

When we turn to the two letters which Paul wrote Timothy, and the letter which he wrote to Titus, we find mention made of journeys or incidents which it is difficult to fit into the journeys of Paul up to the time of this first visit to Rome; and in the Second Letter to Timothy, there are references to his imprisonment and his trial, which are in complete contrast with such references as we have in the Letter to the Philippians. Instead of rejoicing in his situation and giving thanks that through him the Gospel is having such a free course and being glorified, Paul lets Timothy know that his imprisonment now is very severe, for he says, "I suffer hardship unto bonds, as a malefactor." He praises Onesiphorus, of the Church of Ephesus, because he sought him out and was not ashamed of his chains, intimating that it is now dangerous to visit him. He tells Timothy that at the first hearing of his case, none of his friends stood by him, but all forsook him. Nevertheless, the Lord stood by him, and he had opportunity to testify to Christ among the Gentiles.

MYSTERIOUS INTERLUDE

A reasonable inference is that after his two years of a not severe imprisonment at Rome, where he lived in his own hired house, Paul was acquitted of the charges which were preferred against him in the court of Nero. Since he no doubt brought with him a favorable report from Festus, in whose jurisdiction he had appealed to Caesar, there is every reason to believe that Paul would have been acquitted in the court of Caesar at Rome. When he was acquitted, he would be free to go where he pleased. We know that it had long been an ambition of his to preach the Gospel in Spain, which at that time was one of the most important of the Roman provinces. We cannot trace his course with any degree of certainty; but if he was set free and carried out his express purpose of visiting Spain, he probably went first into the west to Spain and then returned to Asia Minor, for we know that it was his purpose to visit friends and churches in that vicinity.

It has been thought by some that Paul was in Spain when Rome was burned by Nero and the great persecution instigated by that monster broke out against the Christians, who were falsely charged with firing the city. This was in the summer of 64 A.D. It has even been suggested that Paul went as far west as Britain. Outside of the Scriptures, there are a number of very noteworthy statements to the effect that between his first and second imprisonments, Paul preached the Gospel in Spain and other countries. One of the most important of these records is that by Clement, the Bishop of Rome, and probably the Clement mentioned in the Letter to the Philippians as one of Paul's fellow-workers. Clement says that Paul preached in the east and west and had gone to the extremity of the west. The natural interpretation of that expression, "the extremity of the west," is Spain. Paul had said in his Letter to the Romans, "Whensoever I take my journey into Spain, I will come to you: for I trust to see you in my journey and to be brought on my way thitherward by you, if first I be somewhat filled with your company." The Muratorian Canon, a New Testament compilation of 179 A.D., states that Luke omits the journey of Paul from Rome to Spain. The Church historian, Eusebius, says it was reported that Paul again went back to proclaim the Gospel and came to Rome the second time and was martyred under Nero. The great preacher of Antioch, Chrysostom, says that Paul, after his residence in Rome, departed to Spain, and Jerome says that Paul was dismissed by Nero that he might preach Christ's Gospel in the west.

We have, therefore, every good reason to believe that Paul was acquitted at his first trial, and then set out on his last missionary journey, preaching the Gospel in Spain and then in Asia Minor. He must have visited the island of Crete, for in his Letter to Titus, Paul speaks of the reason why he left him there. Ephesus, too, must have been visited, for Paul speaks of how he left Trophimus sick at Miletus, not far from Ephesus, and how he left his cloak at Troas, in the house of Carpus. Very likely Corinth, too, was visited for he says that Erastus remained at Corinth. At the end of his letter to Titus, Paul directs Titus to come to him with all diligence to Nicopolis. There were several cities in the ancient world of that name, but it is generally supposed that the Nicopolis where Paul planned to winter was a city of Epirus, on the Adriatic Sea and built by Caesar Augustus to celebrate the naval victory of Actium, 31 B.C., where he defeated the fleets of Mark Antony. Some think that it was at this Nicopolis that Paul was arrested and carried to Rome for his second trial. Because he left his books and cloak behind him at Troas, others have thought that city must have been the place of arrest. Wherever it was, Paul was seized by the Roman authorities, taken to Rome, and subjected to a severe imprisonment. It is not unlikely that his prison was the Mamertine dungeon, where the noble Gallic chief, Vercingetorix, was strangled to death by the order of Julius Caesar, in strange contrast with the usual magnanimity of that soldier and conqueror.

The visitor who knocks on the door hard by the church under the brow of the Capitoline Hill at Rome, finds himself admitted into a narrow, dark stairway. Descending that winding stone stairway, he comes at length to the dismal low arched chamber where it is not improbable the great prisoner of Christ lay bound, waiting to be offered up. Even on an August day, the visitor will feel the dampness of the dungeon and will not wonder that Paul besought Timothy to fetch the cloak which he had left behind him at Troas.

What a cloak the Church of Christ today would weave for her great Apostle! But then, when he lay a prisoner in that dark dungeon, that was the only cloak which Paul could hope to have. He had woven it with his own hands. It had been wet with the brine of the Aegean, yellow with the dust of the Egnatian Way, white with the snows of Galatia and Pamphylia, and crimson with the blood from his own wounds. There, in that dark den, Paul received the courageous and faithful Onesiphorus, who was not ashamed of his chains, was ministered to by Luke, the beloved physician, and wrote his last letter, the Second Letter to Timothy, whom he had left in the Church at Ephesus, exhorting him to stand fast as a servant of Jesus Christ, and beseeching him to come, and to come before winter, for if he did not come before winter, the season of navigation in the Mediterranean would be closed and he would have to wait until the spring; and Paul has a premonition that he will not live to see another spring.

He tells Timothy that he is about to be offered up, and that the time of his departure is at hand, "For I am now ready to be offered and the time of my departure is at hand. I have fought a good fight, I have finished my course, I have kept the faith; henceforth there is laid up for me a crown of righteousness, which the Lord, the righteous judge, shall give me at that day; and not to me only, but unto all them also that love his appearing." None could challenge the statement that Paul had fought a good fight, finished his course and kept the faith. Who ever fought a better fight? Who ever kept the faith more heroically? Who ever finished his course and came to the grave with greater glory and renown? Who ever had a better expectation for the crown of righteousness and the presence of the Lord?

We like to think that Timothy needed no second admonition, and that hurrying over to Troas, he gathered up the books, the parchment and the cloak, took the first ship to Italy, and when he reached Rome, ministered to the last necessities of Paul, walked by his side to the place of execution, and received his final benediction.

When Paul, closely guarded, emerged from the darkness of the Mamertine dungeon, his eyes fell upon the splendid columns, altars, and temples of the Forum. As Paul gazed on those monuments of imperial Roman splendor and dominion, we can be sure that he did not forget what he had once said, how that Christ shall take captivity captive, how He must reign till He hath put all enemies under His feet, and how every knee shall bow of things in heaven, on earth, and under the earth, and every tongue confess that Christ is Lord.

Certain of the great victory of the Captain of his Salvation, and that by the blood of His cross Christ would one day reconcile all things to God, Paul marched forward to his death. Somewhere outside the city walls, perhaps not far from the spot where now the dead sleep beneath the trees in the beautiful Protestant Cemetery, Paul bowed his head to receive the stroke, commending his soul to Christ, we like to think, in the very words which he himself had once heard the martyr Stephen use, "Lord Jesus, receive my spirit."

The headsman's sword flashed for a moment in the sunlight, and Paul had gone to be with Christ. He had once written that to depart and be with Christ was "far better" than to remain. How much better it is, Paul now knows, not in part but even as he is known. There, then, we leave him, "ever with the Lord."

ADDITIONAL RESOURCES FOR YOUR STUDY OF BIBLE CHARACTERS

Sermon Outlines on
Bible Characters (Old Testament)   Compiled by Al Bryant
This collection includes sermon outlines on Old Testament characters from Adam to Samson and Sarah, selected from the writings of such pulpit giants as Jabez Burns, James Hastings and Robert Murray M'Cheyne. They have been selected for their strong scriptural support and solid expository structure. Indexed by subject (Bible Character) and Scriptural references, they will enhance the pulpit ministry and enrich those in the pew.

ISBN 0-8254-2297-3   64 pp.   paperback

Sermon Outlines on
Bible Characters (New Testament)   Compiled by Al Bryant
From the prophetess Anna through the Wise Men who came to worship Jesus, the subjects of these sermon outlines become living, breathing people to preacher and hearer alike. Included are series on the people Jesus profiled in the parables, a unique series on the various facets of the life of Christ, and the life of the Apostle Paul. Included are sermons from pulpit giants like F. E. Marsh, Jabez Burns and other sources.

New insights into how Jesus dealt with individuals will guide preacher and people alike into new understandings of biblical truth.

ISBN 0-8254-2298-1   64 pp.   paperback

Designed for Conquest   Roy L. Laurin
This unique book offers practical help for life's problems. Through the experience of these biblical models, you will discover the secrets which will enable you to be an overcomer, whether enjoying times of plenty or struggling through adversity.

ISBN 0-8254-3139-5   192 pp.   paperback